The First Blitz
in 100
OBJECTS

In memory of my father
Arthur Edward Castle
1930 – 2018

The First Blitz

in 100

OBJECTS

Ian Castle

FRONTLINE
BOOKS

The First Blitz in 100 Objects

This edition published in 2019 by Frontline Books,
An imprint of Pen & Sword Books Ltd.,
Yorkshire - Philadelphia

Copyright © Ian Castle, 2019

HB ISBN 978-1-52673-289-7
PB ISBN 978-1-52676-726-4

CIP data records for this title are available from the British Library

Pen & Sword Books Limited incorporates the imprints of Atlas, Archaeology, Aviation, Discovery, Family History, Fiction, History, Maritime, Military, Military Classics, Politics, Select, Transport, True Crime, Air World, Frontline Publishing, Leo Cooper, Remember When, Seaforth Publishing, The Praetorian Press, Wharncliffe Local History, Wharncliffe Transport, Wharncliffe True Crime and White Owl.

PEN & SWORD BOOKS LTD
47 Church Street, Barnsley, South Yorkshire, S70 2AS, England
E-mail: enquiries@pen-and-sword.co.uk
Website: www.pen-and-sword.co.uk

Or
PEN AND SWORD BOOKS
1950 Lawrence Rd, Havertown, PA 19083, USA
E-mail: Uspen-and-sword@casematepublishers.com

For more information on our books, please visit
www.frontline-books.com, email info@frontline-books.com
or write to us at the above address.

Typeset in 10/14pt Adobe Caslon by Aura Technology and Software Services, India
Printed and bound in India by Replika Press Pvt. Ltd.

Contents

Introduction

The idea for *The First Blitz in 100 Objects* was first suggested to me by my publisher, Martin Mace of Frontline Books. It was an interesting proposition and not one I had considered before. The first question was whether I thought there would be enough 'objects' to fulfil the title. Over the years I have spent researching and writing about the German First World War air raids on Britain, I have come across references to many interesting reminders of this First Blitz, this Forgotten Blitz – but were there enough to fill a book? I started to compile a list of objects that immediately came to mind and my publisher did likewise. It looked promising. I then discussed the idea with others and more suggestions and ideas came forward. I soon discovered that 100 Objects would not be a problem, the problem would be what to leave out!

The next question I had to address was what actually defined an 'object' for the purposes of this project. To reflect on the richness of the offerings, I decided on an open interpretation. I have included locations where significant incidents occurred, graves and plaques that tell of heroic sacrifice within the overall story of the First Blitz, and, of course, some of the weapons that played a role in the war. The impact of individual actions on the Home Front also provided me with 'objects', as did the strength demonstrated by those whose businesses suffered from bombing but who carried on in the face of adversity. There are the relics from crashed airships and the thriving souvenir trade that grew as a result. Some 'objects' reflect the humour the British people displayed during this dark period in the nation's history, and there is space for the more quirky items too: the cartoon-decorated animal bone dropped from a Zeppelin, a bird killed in a raid and stuffed, a collar that saved a man's life and even a board game based on the Zeppelin raids, available while raids still threatened Britain. By using 'objects' such as these it has been possible to explore the impact the First Blitz had on the British public and the combatants of both sides.

Rather than group the 'objects' together under categories, I decided to let them run chronologically so the reader can easily follow the course of the war through the story each 'object' tells. It is a fascinating story and I hope the varied selection of 'objects' reveal many lesser-known aspects of the First Blitz to a much wider audience.

I completed this project in 2018 at the end of a four-year period of centenary commemorations. During that time many previously neglected memorials up and down the country have received welcome attention, and with them new plaques provide a proud source of remembrance. The 'objects' included in this book also show the great variety of ways in which the British people chose to remember the impact those early air raids had on the nation. The previously unthinkable horror had happened – the aerial bombing of civilians in their homes. Yet rather than be cowed by their experience, the British people in general displayed a remarkable courage and resilience in the face of adversity that pre-dated by a quarter of a century the acknowledged 'Blitz spirit' of the Second World War. I hope this book goes some way to reflect that spirit.

Ian Castle, December 2018

Acknowledgments

When embarking on a project of this nature it is impossible to make a success of it without the help of many people. I have been amazed by the response I received from people up and down the country who I contacted out of the blue but who wholeheartedly embraced the project and enabled me to gain access to objects and items that might otherwise have eluded me. A number of museums have been extremely helpful and I would like to thank Nikki Braunton at the Museum of London, Sheila Moss King at The Pennoyer Centre, Jacqueline Smith from the Royal Crown Derby Museum, Chris Langdon at the Southend Museum, John Chapman at Leiston's Long Shop Museum, Sue Walker White at Dereham's Bishop Bonner's Cottage Museum and Bob Goodrick at Tangmere Military Aviation Museum. Clara Morgan at Museums Sheffield, Trevor Neale from Stow Maries Great War Aerodrome and Bryce Caller from the London Museum of Water and Steam also helped greatly by giving permission to reproduce photographs from their collections, while Michael Kelly at the Chatham Drill Hall Library proved an enthusiastic guide.

I am also grateful for the help I have received from a number of individuals. Dr Hamish McLaren, Thomas Genth and Geoffrey Wyncoll all helped with family items. A chance meeting with Charles Dace gained me access to the amazing relic of the First Blitz at Wrotham Park, and Paul Bessemer, a liveryman of the Worshipful Company of Ironmongers, smoothed my path to see their relic of a German raid, as did Neil Wells at the Rochford Hundred Golf Club. John Rochester at the Royal Hospital, Chelsea, gave me access to their archives and Sue Wardle of Emmanuel Holcombe School took photos of the school's unique First Blitz relic and others photos in the village. Peter Daniel opened the door to Clarendon College, Ballarat, where Simone Andrews was most helpful, and Dr Hugh Hunt put me in contact with his cousin Antony Anderson, who was able to help with a family photograph. Email communications with Marc Carlson at the University of Tulsa proved fruitful and I would like to thank James Pasby at the North East War Memorials Project as well as Chris Laidler and Stephen Walker from the Goole First World War Research Group. Both groups do sterling work and provided me with photographs that I have used, as did Gerry Ryder of the Rainhill Civic Society Heritage Group, Charley Gosse of The Aero Conservancy and Andy Tregenza and Steve Littlejohn of Arundel Militaria.

Other individuals I would like to express my thanks to are James Brazier, Mick Davis, Lynne Dyer, Neil Gordon-Lee, Julian Evan-Hart, Les Haigh, Phil Jarrett, Kevin Kelly, Chris Kolonko, Rob Langham, Tom Marshall, Robert Mitchell, Bev Parker, Thorsten Pietsch, Paul Reed, Kevin Ryan, Marton Szgeti and Moritz Adolf Trappe, who all provided images for inclusion in this book. And special thanks go to my long-time friend Mark Lawley, who stopped off to take photos for me while cycling from John o'Groats to Land's End!

I am indebted also to my good friend David Marks, whose unparalleled collection I have relied heavily on, also to Steve Smith whose enthusiasm for the project saw him trekking around Norfolk on my behalf, to Historic Military Press for access to their collection of images and to Martin Mace, my publisher for his unbounded enthusiasm for the project.

Finally, I would like to express my great gratitude to Ian Campbell in Australia. We have never met but Ian's support, advice and sharp eye during the writing process are valued greatly – and he has a family connection with the subject. His great uncle, who served in the Royal Navy, visited the wreck of Zeppelin L 15 in 1916 and obtained some souvenirs of this dramatic incident in the history of the First Blitz. Souvenirs of this type, acquired by both civilians and service personnel alike, were highly sought after at the time, and still are today. Those in my own collection convinced me to undertake this project. Except where otherwise credited, photographs in the book are from this collection.

I am extremely grateful to all those who have happily and enthusiastically contributed to this work, it would never have been the book it is now without their help.

Ian Castle
www.IanCastleZeppelin.co.uk

1

German Airship Girders

Zeppelin v Schütte-Lanz

In the years leading up to the outbreak of the First World War, Germany was home to the leading exponents of rigid airship design. Count Ferdinand von Zeppelin led the way when he launched his first airship, LZ 1, in July 1900. Originally constructing his airship frameworks of aluminium girders, Zeppelin switched to duralumin late in 1914. Duralumin, an alloy of aluminium (95%), copper (4%), magnesium (0.5%)

and manganese (0.5%), maintained the strength of aluminium but offered a reduction in weight, a great benefit in airship construction. After the flight of LZ 1, Count Zeppelin appointed Ludwig Dürr as his chief engineer, who two years later designed the triangular section girders that featured in all subsequent Zeppelins.

Count Zeppelin's work was not without its setbacks and the destruction in July 1908 of his

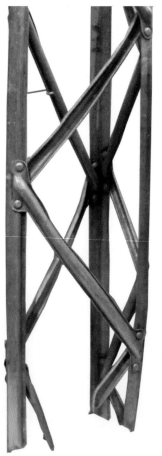

A section of Zeppelin girder structure made of duralumin, an aluminium alloy. The configuration of the girders varied in different areas of the airship but all retain this familiar look.

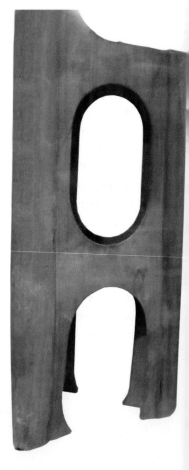

Schütte-Lanz airships differed from Zeppelins in that they were constructed of plywood girders, built up from three or more layers of veneer between 0.5 and 2mm thick and glued together. Using this process the laminate could be formed into different profiles.

fourth Zeppelin, LZ 4, while attempting a flight of 24 hours, drew the attention of Johann Schütte, a professor of theoretical naval architecture. He wrote to Zeppelin suggesting improvements to his design but when the Count paid no heed, he secured backing from two wealthy industrialists, Dr Karl Lanz and August Röchling, to build rigid airships to his own designs. Schütte-Lanz airships had a streamlined profile in advance of their rival's designs but, in a departure from Zeppelin construction, they had a framework of plywood girders, formed of three or more veneers, each between 0.5mm to 2mm thick. Although treated, the wood remained vulnerable to water absorption. For the German Navy this was a major issue. Peter Strasser, commander of the Naval Airship Division, certainly had little time for them. During the war he stated: 'I consider it would be a mistake to build more Schütte-Lanz ships, for experience has thoroughly demonstrated that wood is an unsuitable material for airship construction, because it weakens and breaks with even a moderate degree of humidity.'[1]

Although the two companies remained rivals, Zeppelin dominated. Between 1914 and 1918 the Zeppelin Company built 91 airships while Schütte-Lanz constructed 20, of which only 17 saw service. By the time German airships loomed menacingly over the cities, towns and villages of Britain, the Count's name had already become synonymous with airships, as it remains to this day.

The Zeppelin and Schütte-Lanz girders shown here are in the collection of the Zeppelin Museum in Friedrichshafen, Germany.

A souvenir from SL 11

Undoubtedly the most well-known of the Schütte-Lanz airships was SL 11, the first German airship shot down over mainland Britain. Attacked by Lieutenant William Leefe Robinson flying a B.E.2c aircraft, the explosive and incendiary bullets fired from his Lewis gun ignited SL 11's hydrogen and the flaring, burning wreck crashed on farmland at the village of Cuffley in Hertfordshire. Because the main component of the airship was wood, little survived the conflagration (see Object 56). It is remarkable therefore that this piece of wooden girder did. It came into the possession of Irene Ruth Garstin, a young women living in Highgate, north London. To acquire a piece this size meant she must have visited the crash site very early in the morning or perhaps had influential friends as the site was soon cordoned off and sightseers kept back to prevent removal of objects such as this from the wreckage.

This piece, which is now in a private collection, measures about 17cm by 21cm and is from a larger girder section constructed in a zig-zag pattern. Girders of this 'flat' type were used throughout the framework alongside the more 'rounded' type seen on the previous page, the different types designed to deal with the varying stresses the airships were subjected to in flight.

A section of a zig-zag pattern Schütte-Lanz girder, this one from the wreckage of SL 11. Both this type and that shown on the previous page were used alongside each other in the construction process. (Photo courtesy of Neil Gordon-Lee)

2

1-pdr 'Pom-Pom'

The Gresham College gun – an early defender of London

At the beginning of August 1914, London was defenceless against aerial attack, but four days after the declaration of war the capital received three 1-pdr guns. Mounted on top of Government buildings in Whitehall, they remained London's sole gunnery defence until October of that year, when a deputation led by the Lord Mayor of the City of London succeeded in securing ten more guns. There were two 3-inch guns, three 6-pdrs and five more 1-pdrs; one of the latter was placed at Gresham College, on the corner of Gresham Street and Basinghall Street, and is now part of the Imperial War Museum collection.

Constructed by Vickers, Son & Maxim, the 1-pdr gun had earned the nickname 'pom-pom' from the sound it made when fired. The 1-pdr Mark II at Gresham College had originally seen service in South Africa but, back in Britain, after being fitted with a high-angle pedestal for its new anti-aircraft role, it returned to service in 1914. Even so, few in authority had much confidence in its ability to destroy Zeppelins. A report issued at the end of the war was rather damning as to their effectiveness: 'The pom-poms were of very little value. There was no shrapnel available for them, and the shell provided for them would not burst on aeroplane fabric but fell back to earth as solid projectiles.'[2] But at a time early in the war when anti-aircraft guns were in short supply at least the sound of its rapid fire offered some reassurance to the population of London.

The 1-pdr at Gresham College only came into action once while in the capital. On the night of 8 September 1915, Kapitänleutnant Heinrich Mathy steered Zeppelin L 13 over Bloomsbury and followed a course across London. The 1-pdr at Gresham College and another positioned at the Cannon Street Hotel both opened fire at 10.45pm, the first of the central London guns to do so. Both were in action for 11 minutes and each fired 11 rounds. The officer commanding the Gresham College gun that night, sub-Lieutenant Charles ffoulkes, Royal Naval Volunteer Reserve (RNVR), later became the first curator of the Imperial War Museum.[3] Later that month the gun was transferred to a position at Shingle Street on the Suffolk coast, before relocating again in October 1915 to Ipswich, then to Chatham in February 1917.

This 1-pdr Mark II was positioned on the roof of Gresham College, London, in October 1914, but a year passed before it first came into action. (Courtesy of Chris Kolonko)

A 1-pdr shell. The complete shell measures 16cm (6.3 inches).

3

20lb Hales Bomb

The first bomb to destroy a Zeppelin

A bomb designed in 1913 by Frederick Marten Hale of the Cotton Powder Company at Faversham, Kent, known as the Hales bomb, made a significant impact in the early months of the war. The 20lb bomb contained an Amatol explosive charge weighing 4.5lbs contained in a steel case measuring 21 inches in length. The Royal Naval Air Service (RNAS) station at Eastchurch on the Isle of Sheppey, Kent, was a hotbed of experimental work, and its proximity enabled Marten Hale to work with the pilots there, carrying out tests that suggested his bomb could be effective against airships.

In considering the threat offered by German airships in the months leading up to the outbreak of war, the Admiralty defined its view on air defence: 'Whilst passive measures are useful as safeguards, the real key to the situation will be found to lie in a vigorous and offensive attack on the enemy's air-sheds, &c., and on his aircraft before they reach these shores.'[4]

Between September and December 1914, the RNAS carried out a number of attacks on these targets. Firstly, against the Zeppelin sheds at Cologne and Düsseldorf, secondly, against the Zeppelin works at Friedrichshafen, and finally an attack by seaplanes (more correctly floatplanes) against the Zeppelin base at Nordholz near Cuxhaven. The weapon employed against these targets was the 20lb Hales bomb.

Of the raids that reached their targets, the first on the Düsseldorf shed in September failed despite the pilot dropping all three of his bombs: one exploded about 100 feet short of the shed and the other two failed to detonate. A second raid on Düsseldorf, however, succeeded spectacularly. On 8 October 1914, Lieutenant Reginald Marix, piloting a Sopwith Tabloid and carrying just two Hales bombs, hit the shed and destroyed Army Zeppelin Z IX inside. The following month three Avro 504 aircraft, each loaded with four Hales bombs, made a daring attack on Friedrichshafen, but their bombs failed to cause significant damage to the works. Finally, on 25 December 1914, the attack on Nordholz took place. Seven seaplanes, each carrying three Hales bombs, reached the target area but a thick mist blanketed the ground and none of the pilots were able to locate the Zeppelin sheds.

Although the raids were not completely successful, the destruction of Zeppelin Z IX had proved the effectiveness of the Hales bomb, a fact confirmed in June 1915 when Flight sub-Lieutenant Reginald Warneford, RNAS, dropped six 20lb Hales bombs on Zeppelin LZ 37, destroying her in mid-air. (see Object 14)

A 20lb Hales bomb, the type favoured by the RNAS during the late 1914 raids on Zeppelin bases in Germany.

One of the 20lb Hales bombs that failed to detonate when dropped during the raid on the Düsseldorf Zeppelin shed in September 1914. (Collection DEHLA)

Avro 504 aircraft preparing to take off from Belfort in France to attack the Zeppelin factory at Friedrichshafen, Germany, in November 1914. Each aircraft carried four 20lb Hales bombs.

4

The First Bomb on Britain

At about 10.45am on Christmas Eve 1914, the first German bomb dropped over Britain fell on Dover in Kent. The population of the town was busy preparing for the festive holiday when an aeroplane, a Friedrichshafen FF 29, appeared overhead and released a single 10kg high-explosive bomb, seemingly aimed at Dover Castle.

The bomb missed the castle, landing about 300 yards from its outer earthen ramparts, in the kitchen garden of a house at the corner of Leyburn Road and Taswell Street owned by auctioneer Thomas Terson. A son of Martyn Mowll, a prominent Dover solicitor, was in Taswell Street with a friend when they heard a whirring sound and, looking up, saw a falling object with smoke trailing behind it. Newspapers reported: 'Immediately the bomb hit the ground there was a terrible explosion, and the earth shot up to a great height, covering him, although he was standing about 25 yards away.'[5] The explosion gouged a crater in Mr Terson's cabbage patch, wrecked his summerhouse and smashed the glass in his greenhouses. The force of the blast seared across the adjoining garden at St James's Rectory. Rev. T. B. Watkins and his family were out but his gardener, John Banks, was clambering in a tree cutting evergreen branches to decorate the church for the Christmas service, while the cook was busy in the kitchen. The blast swept Banks from the tree but fortunately he fell into bushes, which broke his fall. A fragment of the bomb struck the tree just above where he had been.

A postcard issued at the time showing a fragment of the first bomb dropped on Britain from the air, which the Dover Anti-aircraft Corps presented to the King. (The David Marks Collection)

Broken window glass showered the cook but she was also unhurt, and many other windows nearby were smashed by the concussion. Eager souvenir

Plaque erected by the Dover Society and placed at the corner of Taswell Street and Taswell Close, Dover.

hunters quickly appeared, keen to recover fragments of the bomb, which had travelled up to 100 yards from the point where it exploded.

After the raid, and recognising the significance of the moment, members of the Dover Anti-aircraft Corps secured a small fragment of the bomb, which they had mounted and presented to the King. It formed part of the Royal Collection until loaned to the Imperial War Museum in 1936, where it remains. A plaque erected by the Dover Society and placed on a wall at the corner of Taswell Street and Taswell Close reminds passers-by that the first bomb dropped on Britain fell 'near this spot'.

Graves of Britain's First Air Raid Victims
Great Yarmouth, Norfolk
The first casualties of the First Blitz

The first Zeppelin raid on Britain took place on Tuesday, 19 January 1915. Two Zeppelins crossed the Norfolk coast, with one attacking Great Yarmouth and the other dropping bombs on various towns and villages before making its main attack on King's Lynn. This Zeppelin raid caused the first deaths in Britain by bombs dropped by aircraft of any kind.

Kapitänleutnant Hans Fritz, commanding Zeppelin L 3, had approached Great Yarmouth from the north. Having commenced bombing the town at 8.25pm, his third bomb struck with devastating effect. The blast tore off the front of St Peter's Villa at No. 25 St Peter's Plain, the home of Edward Ellis. He was at home but the rest of his family were away in Cornwall at the time. Mr. Ellis was at the back of the house when the bomb exploded and was lucky to suffer only cuts to his head and legs. Out in the street others were not so fortunate. Directly opposite Mr. Ellis' house, Samuel Smith, a 53-year-old shoemaker, was at his workshop having just finished for the day, and 72-year-old Martha Taylor was returning home from buying food for supper – she lived with her twin sister at Drake's Buildings, its narrow entrance also opposite Mr Ellis' house. The bomb killed both Samuel Smith and Martha Taylor at the same instant. At first, those who rushed to help thought Martha's body was a pile of discarded rags but then they discovered the truth. The blast had ripped off part of an arm and slashed open her left side from shoulder to hip, leaving her organs 'practically destroyed'. They discovered Smith in the passage leading to his workshop. The policemen who found his body reported that his 'skull had been nearly blown away, and the brain stripped from the base of the skull'. [6] Samuel Smith and Martha Taylor, just going about their normal lives, became the first victims of Germany's air campaign against Britain.

In 2012, Great Yarmouth Local History and Archaeological Society unveiled a plaque on No. 25 St Peter's Plain commemorating the bomb that exploded in front of the house claiming the lives of Britain's first air raid fatalities. Samuel Smith was buried in Yarmouth Old Cemetery, Kitchener Road, and Martha Taylor lies in the Caister Cemetery on Ormesby Road.

It is perhaps worth noting that a plaque in Sheringham records that a bomb dropped on the town that same night by Zeppelin L 4 was 'The First Bomb to be dropped on Britain in World War One'. This is incorrect. The first bomb, as we have seen, dropped by an aeroplane fell on Dover on 24 December 1914. If the sign intended to refer to the first Zeppelin bomb then it is also incorrect. Samuel Smith and Martha Taylor were both already dead, killed by the third bomb dropped on Great Yarmouth by L 3, before Zeppelin L 4 dropped its first bomb on Sheringham.

A close-up of the inscription on Samuel Smith's grave. (Courtesy of Steve Smith)

The simple grave of Martha Taylor in Caister Cemetery, with a plaque added around the time of the centenary of her death. (Courtesy of Steve Smith)

The grave of Samuel Smith in Yarmouth Old Cemetery. Samuel was buried in the same grave as his sister, who died in 1905. (Courtesy of Steve Smith)

THE GERMAN AIR RAID ON GREAT YARMOUTH, JANUARY 19th, 1915.
MR. ELLIS WOUNDED BY A BOMB, AND HIS RUINED HOUSE, AT LANCASTER ROAD CORNER,
ST. PETER'S PLAIN.

The destruction caused by the bomb that killed Samuel Smith and Martha Taylor. Samuel's workshop was the building in the centre of the photograph, while Martha's home in Drake's Buildings was down a narrow alleyway between the workshop and the light-coloured building on the left. She was only a few yards from home when the bomb exploded. (The David Marks Collection)

The front of St Peter's Villa, damaged by the same bomb that killed Samuel Smith and Martha Taylor. The owner of the house, Edward Ellis, was inside at the time and escaped with just cuts to his head and legs.

Glass from St Mary's Church
Snettisham, Norfolk
A souvenir of a narrow escape

During the first Zeppelin raid on the night of 19 January 1915, Zeppelin L 4 came inland over the north Norfolk coast. At about 10.40pm she approached the village of Snettisham. Earlier that evening the Rev. I. W. Charlton, vicar of the impressive 14th-century St Mary's Church, had hosted a meeting at the vicarage, located on the north side of the church. The Rev. Charlton, his wife and a friend were now alone when they heard the sound of what they thought was an aeroplane. Leaving the lights burning in the vicarage, they went out into the garden to locate the source of the noise and, possibly attracted by those lights, saw 'the outline of a Zeppelin, hovering over the church and Vicarage'. The Rev. Charlton continues:

'No sooner had we identified it as probably a German airship, than suddenly all doubt was dispelled by a long, loud, hissing sound; a confused streak of light; and a tremendous crash. The next moment was made up of apprehension, relief, and mutual enquiries, and then all was dark and still, as the sound of the retiring Zeppelin speedily died away.'[7]

Fortunately for the Rev. Charlton and those accompanying him, the bomb landed in a meadow on the opposite side of the church, the building shielding them from any flying fragments. If the bomb had fallen just a few yards more to the north then the impact on the church could have been highly destructive; as it was it escaped quite lightly. Holcombe Ingleby, the MP for King's Lynn, described the bomb's

A piece of stained glass from one of the shattered windows of St Mary's Church, Snettisham. (Courtesy of Moritz Adolf Trappe)

ZEPPELIN RAID,

JAN. 19th, 1915.

Pane of Glass

FROM

Snettisham Church,

Norfolk.

A postcard of St Mary's Church after the raid; it clearly shows the damage caused to the windows by the bomb dropped from Zeppelin L 4. (The David Marks Collection)

impact: '… the force of the explosion was so great that most of the windows on the south and east sides of the church were blown in, together with some of the stonework of the mullions. Tablets in this part of the church were knocked down and other damage done.'[8]

The story of the bomb is remembered locally but it has been claimed that St Mary's was the first church in Britain damaged by aerial bombing. In fact that dubious honour belongs to St Peter's in Great Yarmouth, damaged earlier that evening by the bomb that exploded in St Peter's Plain (see Object 5). Visitors who came to see the bomb damage collected fragments of the shattered windows as souvenirs and one such piece from a private collection is shown along with a postcard illustrating the damage to the church.

Crested China

Popular souvenirs of the First Blitz

In the years preceding the First World War, the growth of railway travel led to an increase in domestic tourism. These new travellers sought mementos of their trips and crested china proved a hugely popular souvenir. These small white porcelain models, which came in all shapes, sizes and designs, each bearing heraldic crests of the places visited, adorned the mantelpieces of homes the length and breadth of Britain.

At the beginning of the war there was a strong belief in Germany that bombing raids on Britain would have a significant effect on the nation's morale. Paul Behncke, Deputy Chief of the German Naval Staff, believed that attacks on London and its environs could 'cause panic in the population which may possibly render it doubtful that the war can be continued'.[9] Considering attacks on other targets too he concluded: 'In general, air attacks … particularly with airships, promise considerable material and moral results.'

But Germany had misjudged the mood of the British people. Those early air raids did not

BELOW LEFT: A crested china souvenir based on an incendiary bomb dropped on Maldon by naval Zeppelin L 6. These were popular collectable items and were available all over Britain. This one was sold in Worthing, Sussex, a place never bombed during the war. (Courtesy of David Marks)

BELOW RIGHT: The inscription on the base of the Worthing souvenir bomb, commemorating the bombs dropped on Maldon. (Courtesy of David Marks)

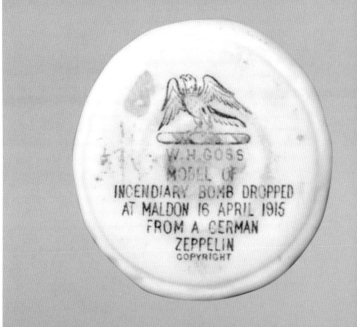

shatter the morale of the people as Germany had expected, and if your family and home were untouched by the bombs then a raid became a thrilling spectacle. People would go out to watch the Zeppelins, they would congregate around any fires that broke out and, when daylight came, whole families would visit the bomb craters to pose for photographs. In April 1915, after Zeppelin raids on Maldon in Essex by Navy Zeppelin L 6, and Bury St Edmunds in Suffolk by Army Zeppelin LZ 38, the crested china manufacturers saw an opportunity and began producing models of the incendiary bombs that had fallen on those towns. The models were surprisingly accurate, with the Maldon bombs representing the type dropped by the Navy Zeppelins and the Bury St Edmunds version showing those dropped by Army Zeppelins. Such was the enthusiasm for these models that their sale was not limited to the two places bombed and versions with different heraldic crests for towns and cities all over the country appeared for sale. Many a household also displayed crested china Zeppelins alongside the bombs. It can hardly have been the reaction to aerial bombing that Germany had expected.

ABOVE LEFT: This bomb, sold in the City of London, represents an incendiary bomb dropped on Bury St Edmunds by army Zeppelin LZ 38.

ABOVE RIGHT: The underside of the City of London souvenir bomb, confirming it was modelled on a bomb dropped on Bury St Edmunds.

A crested china Zeppelin alongside another version of the LZ 38 incendiary bomb. Although Germany anticipated her bombs causing panic in Britain's towns and cities, their populations unexpectedly became keen buyers of souvenirs of the raids.

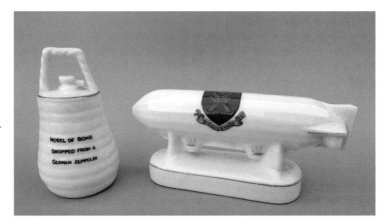

A typical crowd gathered around a Zeppelin bomb crater posing for photographs. This mixed group of military and civilians had come to see a crater at Maldon, Essex, in April 1915. (The David Marks Collection)

The effects of an incendiary bomb on shops in Bury St Edmunds, an incident that led to the manufacture of souvenir china models of this type of bomb.

Souvenir Postcard of a Raid on Britain

The first German Army aeroplane over Britain

In the early months of Germany's aerial campaign against Britain there was no attempt to impose censorship on the reporting of the raids. Throughout January and April 1915, extremely detailed newspaper coverage appeared, naming streets where bombs exploded, interviewing eyewitnesses and providing sketch maps of the routes taken by the raiders. One raid, made by a single aeroplane on 16 April 1915, which dropped bombs on Sittingbourne and Faversham in Kent, led to the publication of a unique souvenir – a picture postcard depicting a map of the raid.

A lone Albatros BII of the army's *Feldflieger Abteilung Nr. 41*, crewed by Oberleutnant Freiherr Dietrich von Kanne and his pilot, Offizierstellvertreter Karl Ritter, set out from Gits, south-east of Ostend, and headed across the English Channel towards Kent. Having

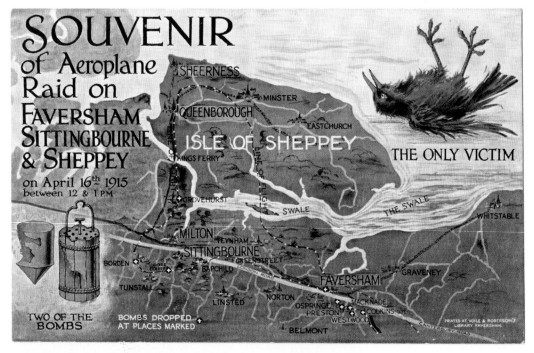

The unique postcard published in Faversham to commemorate the air raid of 16 April 1915. This is to the best of my knowledge the only postcard printed showing the route taken by a German raider over Britain. (Courtesy of James Brazier)

passed over Faversham, Ritter approached Sittingbourne and released five bombs.

At 12.30pm Ritter and von Kanne returned to Faversham, where they dropped five more bombs on the south side of the town.

The first landed in the grounds of The Mount Military Hospital, followed by one in Ashford Road, close to the junction with the London Road. The next landed in a field at Preston village, followed by bombs in an orchard on Macknade Farm and one to the south-east of the town, at Colkins hop gardens.

When von Kanne and Ritter arrived back in Belgium they could rightly claim the honour of being the first army aircraft to bomb Britain, for which they were both awarded the Iron Cross 1st Class, although their claim to have bombed Greenwich in London may have helped!

The postcard illustrating this raid, printed in Faversham, not only indicates the route taken by the German airmen (although the reports of the raid are not always clear), but also gives sketches of two types of bomb dropped and an image of the only victim of the raid – a blackbird, which was blasted from an apple tree at Sittingbourne. There would, however, not be another postcard like this – the following month saw the introduction of reporting restrictions. The other postcard shown, also printed in Faversham, is of the incendiary bomb dropped at The Mount Hospital, which is possibly one of the types the artist tried to replicate on the postcard.

Another postcard published in Faversham, this one showing a damaged Carbonit 4.5kg incendiary bomb. The caption states it is the bomb dropped in the grounds of The Mount Military Hospital. (Courtesy of James Brazier)

9

The Southend Standard

Newspaper reporting before the enforcement of Press restrictions

During the early months of the war, Press reporting of air raids was open and detailed, but the Government became concerned that this was handing useful intelligence to the Germans. To restrict this flow of information, the Government issued a D. Notice (Defence Notice – an official request to editors not to publish articles on specified subjects) on 5 May 1915. The purpose of D.206 was to prevent the publication of news 'likely to cause needless alarm or distress among the civil population'. It informed editors that unofficial reports of raids were not to be published prior to the printing of the official account, and that no mention was to be made of the route taken by enemy aircraft or the amount of damage inflicted. D. Notices were not legally enforceable, but editors were expected to follow their advice. The newspaper coverage of the first raid after issuing D.206 (Southend-on-Sea, 10 May), however, was still revealing. A senior intelligence officer at the War Office, General George Cockerill, monitored the coverage the following day and on 12 May voiced his concerns over the revelation in some reporting that there was an explosives depot at Canvey Island.

It can only be wondered, therefore, how General Cockerill reacted the day after he submitted his report when a local newspaper, the *Southend Standard*, printed an 18-page special supplement comprehensively telling the story of the raid with a level of detail that has never been surpassed.

Following further Zeppelin raids that month, on 27 May newspaper editors received a reminder of their responsibilities as reporting continued to offer significant detail. But these niceties came to end four days later when the first Zeppelin bombs fell on London. Before the sun had risen the following morning, the Press Bureau issued new, firm directives. There would be no more free reporting of the raids, no more naming places bombed, or towns and villages passed by the raiders. Later that day D. Notice 217 followed. 'In the public interest and to prevent the publication of information useful to the enemy, it has been decided that nothing may appear in the Press in regard to raids by enemy aircraft except the official statements issued by the Government.'[10]

Later, newspapers were allowed to report on the raids after publishing the official statements, but these were without reference to the places affected, merely including references such as a 'northern town' or on the 'east coast'.

The *Southend Standard* supplement marked the high-water mark in air raid reporting, although no doubt the Government at the time would not agree.

The front page of the 18-page air raid supplement issued by the *Southend Standard* on 13 May 1915.
This publication provided the most detailed account of the first Southend Zeppelin raid ever published.
(Historic Military Press)

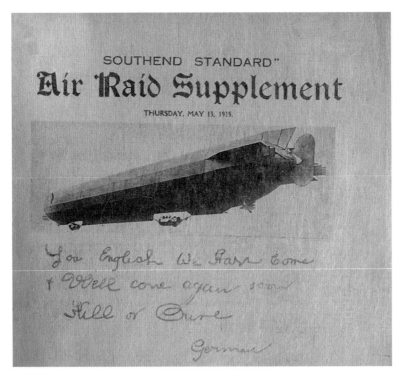

The front page of the special edition included a copy of a message scrawled on a piece of card and dropped from the Zeppelin. Recovered from a garden in the town, it read: 'You English, we have come and will come again soon. Kill or Cure.' The message was signed, 'German'.

Crowds gather outside the Cromwell Board Residence in London Road, Southend-on-Sea, to view the damage to the property caused by an incendiary bomb, one of many individual incidents described in detail in the *Standard*'s special air raid edition. (Historic Military Press)

AIR RAID OVER SOUTHEND.

ONE WOMAN MURDERED.

Houses Burnt Out: Others Seriously Damaged.

Press Association message passed by Press Censor on Monday:—

Two Zeppelins visited Southend and district early to-day and dropped numerous bombs.

One woman was killed and some property set alight.

Official communiqué from the Army Head-quarters issued in Berlin on Monday:—

One of our airships early this morning dropped some bombs on the fortified place of Southend, at the estuary of the Thames.

Southend was the scene of the first air raid on this country, when an aeroplane (some say there were two) was discovered at the Thames mouth on Christmas morning, chased along our banks for some miles, and finally headed away to the North Sea over Wakering. Its fate is unknown, but there are circumstantial statements that the subsequent finding of the dead body of an aviator and his machine near these shores affords the clue to the mystery.

Now Southend-on-Sea has the melancholy satisfaction of knowing that nearly six months afterwards it was visited by the most formidable effort yet made from the air upon this country. Sunday was a beautiful day, with a strong easterly wind, which would favour a quick passage across the North Sea. The many thousands who thoroughly enjoyed the sunshine little thought as they went to bed what the sleeping hours would bring. The night was dark, and in the early morning the sky was streaked with small clouds, with a basi-ness which made it difficult to detect anything moving in the sky above. It was at such a favourable juncture that the blow was struck and fell upon the unfortified watering-place of Southend. The affair occupied so few minutes in its happening that it is not easy to judge the route of the aircraft, give number or description, or to say with certainty what the objective was. Indeed the varied accounts given of what was seen illustrate very vividly the hurried nature of the visit and the indefinite impressions that were conveyed. It is safe to say Southend was twice visited; on the onward and the return journey, which were very closely connected. Apparently the aircraft stopped short about Bread and Cheese Hill, Thundersley, hurling incendiary bombs on that district and South Benfleet, and then turned back at full speed towards the North Sea, perhaps because the effect of her work at Southend was being quickly observed. Independent accounts all agree that operations

began about 2.45; the first call being made to the fire brigade at 2.49. Mr. Flaxman's timber yard and shops were then well alight as the result of an incendiary bomb; another also striking the dwelling house and inflicting considerable damage. Just previously the first explosion was felt; a sharp, almost painful detonation sending many thousands of burgesses straight out of their beds and to the windows, where a whirring noise was heard. It was this shell which possibly struck a house at the rear of 192, York Road East, where the occupants (Mr. and Mrs. Warr) and Corpl. Hanny, of the Border Regiment, and his wife and child, had narrow escapes; a huge hole being made in the back garden and the rear structure seriously damaged. Very shortly afterwards another sharp explosion was heard, and it may be that this was the shell which struck the piece of waste land in front of Ambleside Drive, making a great hole in the ground; the force of the concussion breaking the windows of scores of neighbouring houses. It was quite a sight on Monday morning to see glaziers working as if for very life to re-glaze the ashes before nightfall. There was a third explosive bomb, which crashed through the wood paving of Victoria Avenue opposite the Technical School and embedded itself in concrete without exploding. Another was also thrown at Westborough School playground, and passed through the asphalte without bursting. So much for the enemy's effort at destruction of life by explosives. The attempt to destroy property by means of incendiary bombs was much more fruitful of result, although even then the results were puny contrasted with the personal risk and financial outlay involved. Westcliff and Leigh were peppered with them. Benfleet and Thundersley marked the termination of the raid, and on the return journey further fire bombs were dropped.

From the accounts of eye witnesses and a careful survey of the spots where bombs were dropped, it seems probable that the Zeppelin first arrived from over Foulness, started bomb-dropping near St. Erkenwald's Church, and then stopped over the centre of the town, swaying in the wind. Whilst there a large number of incendiary bombs were fired; the electricity works being the objective. Then the enemy, perhaps having settled her course, passed over Coleman's Estate to North Leigh and on to Thundersley and Benfleet. Hereabouts the anti-aircraft guns awoke to life, and finding the position too hot or having completed her

reconnaissance, or the dawn being at hand, the ship turned and made for the sea as quickly as she could; dropping a large quantity of bombs near Leigh gas works and the marshes as if anxious to get rid of them as quickly as possible. The Zeppelin then came over Southern Southend — the incendiary bomb at the Technical School probably being dropped on the way—and made off to sea without perceptible hindrance. Indeed, some assert it was over an hour before the whirr of an aeroplane told of pursuit.

The type of projectiles was easily ascertained. The explosive bomb near the Technical School was a round steel cylinder, about two feet in diameter. The incendiary bombs are by now well-known to readers; having been made familiar to them in our description of the Maldon raid. A steel tube has affixed to it a steel basin, and at the top a handle of stout wire; the incandescent material being placed round the shaft. It consists of soaked rag, charcoal, and other inflammable constituents, including minute pieces of coal.

The hour chosen was the best possible for the purpose. The darkest hour before the dawn was made more suitable by the cloudy atmosphere, which rendered floating objects in the sky absolutely invisible or only of shadowy, indistinct outlines. The evidence of people who were out at the time suggest that a Zeppelin was employed — the various descriptions used being a vessel the shape of a "sausage," or a "stick of pencil" or a "cigar." These are the descriptive phrases associated in the popular mind with the Zeppelin aloft. Mr. Mason, of Southend Gas Works, gives one of the most intelligible accounts, in the course of which he makes it clear that the aircraft paid a return visit to Southend. There is little to support the theory of a second vessel. As it was, the Zeppelin was flying unusually high. The number of bombs dropped tends to preclude the idea of aeroplanes, because quite a number would have been employed, and the bomb-dropping would have taken place over a wider area. Some there are who say that they could have thrown a stone at the invader, or if they had had a rifle they could have played havoc with it. We prefer to believe that it kept at a comparatively safe distance, and that that was the reason for the comparatively poor results achieved—the murder of one woman (Mrs. Whitwell) in her bed, the destruction of the whole or parts of eleven houses, and the creation of numerous cavities in the ground.

'One woman murdered,' the reporting of the Southend raid begins. The women referred to was Agnes Whitwell, aged 60, who lived at No. 120 North Road. The supplement also included a photo of the house with a hole in the roof where the bomb passed through. (Historic Military Press)

Souvenirs from the Imperial Bazaar
Ramsgate, Kent
Twice damaged by Zeppelin attack

In the early hours of 17 May 1915, Zeppelin LZ 38, commanded by Hauptmann Erich Linnarz, approached the popular seaside town of Ramsgate in Kent. As it passed over the town, four high-explosive and 16 incendiary bombs were released. One of the HE bombs exploded behind a small shop on Albion Hill known as Lilly's Imperial Bazaar, crammed full of souvenirs and all the paraphernalia necessary for a perfect seaside holiday.

The bomb smashed down into the cellar where it exploded. It excavated a crater eight feet deep and 20 feet square, causing chaos inside the shop. The manager, Frederick France, was asleep on the first floor. His window shattered in the blast but he escaped injury; a quantity of children's spades he had piled against the window flew into the room, landed on his bed, serendipitously shielding him from the lethal shards of jagged glass.

Two pieces of Ramsgate crested china sold by the Imperial Bazaar in the town.

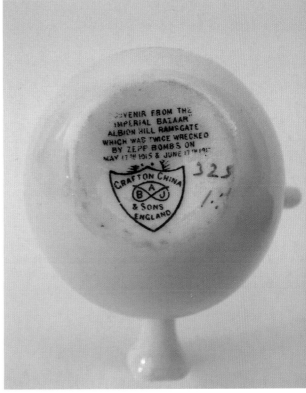

ABOVE LEFT and RIGHT: The inscription on the bottom of each piece gives the dates of the two Zeppelin raids that damaged the shop and were a version specially manufactured for sale at the Imperial Bazaar.

Recognising a chance to cash in on the new-found fame of the shop, a series of postcards were published showing the damage to the premises with Mr France often appearing in them. After repairs were made, 'huge tablets were erected indicating the date of the raid and the effect it had in that particular locality'.[11] As a number of these 'Imperial Bazaar' postcards regularly appear for sale on the collectors' market, it would suggest this was a rather effective marketing ploy.

Exactly 25 months later, on 17 June 1917, another Zeppelin appeared over the town. Zeppelin L 42, commanded by Kapitänleutnant Martin Dietrich, dropped a bomb over the harbour, where by chance it exploded on an ammunition dump on the site of the old fish market: 'A sheet of blood-red flame shot upwards and for hours ammunition of all kinds continued to explode with a tornado of fury.'[12] Just 150 yards away from the centre of this maelstrom, the Imperial Bazaar suffered again.

Once more looking for ways to benefit from its misfortune, this time the Imperial Bazaar focused on the highly popular souvenir crested china that they sold. They now started offering items with a description on the underside: 'Souvenir from the Imperial Bazaar, Albion Hill, Ramsgate. Twice wrecked by Zeppelins May 17th 1915 and June 17th 1917.' That a small shop in a seaside town could become a tourist attraction was another unexpected result of Germany's air campaign against Britain.

Frederick France standing outside the Imperial Bazaar; one of a series of postcards featuring the shop issued after the first raid in May 1915. (The David Marks Collection)

Disruption inside the Imperial Bazaar caused by the Zeppelin bomb in May 1915. (The David Marks Collection)

Sightseers gather to see the damage caused at the back of the Imperial Bazaar.

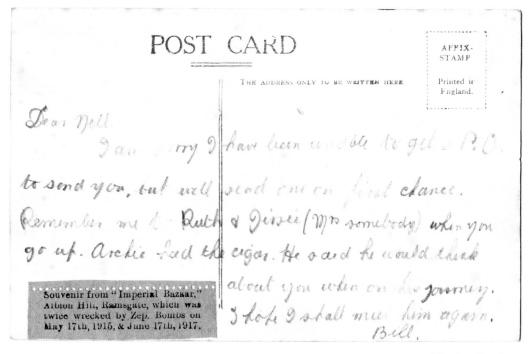

These postcards were produced for sale at the Imperial Bazaar and some carried a small sticker bearing the same words as those on the shop's crested china souvenirs. (The David Marks Collection)

11

16 Alkham Road – London

The first house in London bombed in the First Blitz

When war broke out in August 1914, many thought it would not be long before Germany commenced air attacks on London. In fact the Kaiser, believing like many that the war would soon be over, was reluctant to authorise the bombing of the capital. But with no early end to the war in sight and coming under increasing pressure, he finally relented and approved London as a target. The first raid took place on Monday, 31 May 1915.

Hauptmann Erich Linnarz, commanding Army Zeppelin LZ 38, had already bombed Ipswich, Bury St Edmunds, Southend-on-Sea and Ramsgate in previous raids, now, at about 11pm, he flew over Stoke Newington Station in north London. His approach had gone largely unobserved; no searchlights swept the sky, no guns opened fire. His first bomb, an incendiary, streaked down through the night sky, striking the chimney of No. 16 Alkham Road before smashing through the roof and setting fire to the attic bedroom in this quiet residential street. The house was home to Albert Lovell, a 39-year-old clerk, his wife and their children. That night two guests were sleeping in the room at the top of the house. Dense smoke and fumes quickly filled the room as fiercely burning benzol spread across the floor. After a brief struggle to open the door to the

No. 16 Alkham Road, on the Stoke Newington/ Hackney border in London, the first house in the capital to be bombed by a Zeppelin.

room, Mr Lovell led his guests and family to safety before setting off on his son's bicycle to alert the Fire Brigade.[13] They contained the fire to the upper floor of the house but water from the hoses damaged ceilings and furnishings below.

This historic bomb remained in possession of the Lovell family for many years until becoming part of the Imperial War Museum collection. The house in Alkham Road still stands. In the 1990s the Hackney Society erected plaques in the borough commemorating 'people, places and historic events'. One of those, placed on the old Nevill Arms pub on the corner of Nevill Road and Orpingley Road, stated that it marked the site of the first bomb dropped on London. Unfortunately this was not the correct site, while the date on the plaque was also wrong. In 2015, following discussions with the author of this book, Hackney Council erected a new plaque on 16 Alkham Road in time for the centenary of London's first air raid. Mysteriously, before the council could remove the old one, it disappeared.

A photo taken in the 1930s of the bomb that set fire to the attic bedroom of No. 16 Alkam Road. The family kept the bomb for many years before they subsequently passed it on to the Imperial War Museum.

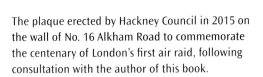

The plaque erected by Hackney Council in 2015 on the wall of No. 16 Alkham Road to commemorate the centenary of London's first air raid, following consultation with the author of this book.

12

Zeppelin Bomb Markers
Gravesend, Kent

Granite stones commemorate the first bombs dropped on Gravesend

On the afternoon of 4 June 1915, Kapitänleutnant Klaus Hirsch, commanding Zeppelin L 10, set out from Germany with orders 'to attack the English south-east coast, target London'. Delayed by strong headwinds, Hirsch felt it was no longer possible to reach London and return under cover of darkness in the short June night, so switched his attention to Harwich. Unknown to him, however, the wind had pushed him southwards. Having located his target, and noting, 'The city of Ipswich, off to the west, was brightly lit and offered an excellent aid to navigation,'[14] Hirsch began dropping his bombs. Rather than the lights of Ipswich, however, Hirsch was actually looking at the lights of London, with the heart of the city in reach just 20 miles away. Instead of his bombs striking Harwich, they actually landed 50 miles to the south-west, on Gravesend.

Before attacking Gravesend, Hirsch appeared over Tilbury, on the north bank of the Thames, from where an anti-aircraft gun engaged L 10. According to a local history:

'Most people had retired to bed, and were awakened by a peculiar noise. Some thought it was a very heavy thunderstorm, others surmised that something very peculiar was happening at Tilbury Docks, but few connected it with a Zeppelin. Yet those who went to their windows and gazed out saw beneath the starry heavens, at a great height, what looked like a silver cigar hovering over Windmill Hill.'[15]

Having satisfied himself that he had found a target, Hirsch ordered the release of the first bombs. Three incendiaries hurtled down on to Windmill Hill, Gravesend, where they burst into flames, sending showers of sparks up into the sky. L 10 then flew over the town towards the Thames, dropping more bombs as it went, severely damaging a house in Windmill Street, demolishing two in Wrotham Road and also wrecking part of the Voluntary Aid Detachment hospital established at the yacht club.

Those first three incendiary bombs on Windmill Hill still have a place in the history of the town. On the north slopes of the hill three cylindrical granite markers were erected on the spot where each of the bombs landed and they remain there to this day.

Commemorative plaque attached to one of the granite markers in 2013.

The three granite markers erected on Windmill Hill, Gravesend, to mark where individual incendiary bombs fell at the start of the raid on the town in June 1915.

After the incendiary bombs dropped on Windmill Hill, L 10 switched to high-explosive bombs. The next bomb severely damaged these two houses in Windmill Street, although there is little sign of the repairs today.

13

The Hull Zeppelin Raid Photographs

Extensive photographic coverage of an air raid

On the night of 6 June 1915, Navy Zeppelin L 9 appeared over the city of Hull shortly before midnight and commenced a devastating raid. The attack lasted 20 minutes, during which time it dropped about 60 bombs, killing 26 people and injuring 40 more.

Advised at 9.30pm of the possibility of a raid, the commander of the Humber Defences, Major-General James Ferrier, ordered the lights out and alerted the police. A prominent local photographer and Special Constable, T. C. Turner, was on duty from 10.30pm until 3am. Through the course of the night Turner, an enterprising man, visited many of the sites where bombs had detonated and made detailed notes. With the return of daylight, he sought and received permission from the military authorities to photograph the places where the bombs had fallen. He toured the streets accompanied by a police sergeant, creating an extraordinary record of the air raid. As well as taking photos in the streets, some of those affected invited him to record the damage inside their homes, too, and he gained important details from many of them. Many of these details annotate the back of his

One of the 46 photographs taken by T. C. Turner in the aftermath of the Hull raid in June 1915. This one, of Walter's Terrace, lists on the reverse the names of four people killed by this bomb: Florence White and her son Isaac, Elizabeth [Eliza] Slade and Alfred Matthews. (Historic Military Press)

photographs. In all he produced 46 photographs and a month after the raid he offered a set to the War Office, at 10s 6d per print, and 2s 6d for duplicates. It appears likely that this is the set now held at the National Archives at Kew in London, although there are only 41 photos in the file.[16] The Hull Museums Collection also holds a set.

Turner, however, was not alone in photographing the bomb-damaged city. The Hull City Engineers' Department took a set of 26 photographs, now held by the Hull History Centre. R. T. Watson was also busy capturing the scenes of destruction too and selling his work to newspapers. As a result, the Hull raid became the most photographed of the First Blitz.

Turner's annotation on the back of the photograph on the previous page of Walter's Terrace off Waller Street, gives the names of four people killed and describes how the bomb left '14 houses demolished or at least made unsafe 4 of which collapsed'. He also described the bomb crater as 18 feet in diameter and seven feet deep. Annotations such as this, when combined with the visual record of the photos, has created a unique record of a single Zeppelin raid.

One of the photographs from the set produced by the Hull City Engineers' Department, showing hosepipes damping down the smouldering ruins of the Edwin Davis & Co store, opposite Holy Trinity Church. (Historic Military Press)

This photograph, believed to be taken by a press photographer, R. T. Watson, appears to show bomb damage in High Street, Hull. (Historic Military Press)

14

Reginald Warneford, VC, Memorial Brompton Cemetery, London

The first British pilot to destroy a Zeppelin in flight

As part of the Admiralty's strategy to attack Zeppelins in their sheds or before they could reach Britain's shores (see Object 3), four RNAS aircraft took off from airfields near Dunkirk in the early hours of 7 June 1915 in an attempt to intercept two Zeppelins making their way home after an aborted raid on England. One of the pilots, Flight sub-Lieutenant Reginald 'Rex' Warneford, encountered Zeppelin LZ 37.

Warneford kept his distance, biding his time until LZ 37 began to descend in preparation for landing. Then he pounced. Warneford dropped six 20lb Hales bombs along LZ 37's back; uncontrollable flames engulfed the stricken Zeppelin as she plummeted to earth. Warneford had become the first pilot to bring down a Zeppelin. The press made Warneford an instant hero and, with the nation in need of a 'good news' story, the King announced the award of the Victoria Cross by telegram the following day. But Warneford was never to receive his medal – he died in a flying accident ten days later. Brought back to London, thousands lined the streets as sailors drew Warneford's coffin on a gun carriage to Brompton Cemetery. He was buried on 22 June surrounded by a crowd estimated at 10,000.

On 11 July 1916, Lord Derby, the Under-Secretary of State for War, unveiled a memorial to Warneford, raised through public subscription by readers of the *Daily Express* newspaper.[17] Erected over the grave, the memorial, designed by the architectural sculptor, Frank Lynn Jenkins, features a relief portrait of Warneford with the words 'Courage – Initiative – Intrepidity'. Lower down, a relief depicts the scene moments after Warneford's bombs exploded, although the artist has depicted a biplane whereas he was flying a single-wing Morane-Saulnier. In his dramatic speech at the unveiling, Lord Derby, with an eye to the value of the memorial as an aid to recruitment, spoke of its importance. Not only would it serve as monument to one who gave his life for his country, Lord Derby explained, but it would also 'furnish for all time and for all generations an incentive to men to set aside their own private interests and their own personal safety, and to lay down, if need be, their lives for their country'.

Reginald Warneford's grave in Brompton Cemetery, London. The money to pay for the impressive memorial standing over the grave was raised by readers of the *Daily Express* newspaper.

Warneford's flag-draped coffin is drawn into Brompton Cemetery on a gun carriage accompanied by men of the RNAS on 22 June 1915.

Flight sub-Lieutenant Reginald Warneford, RNAS, the first pilot to destroy a Zeppelin in the air. Warneford was 23 years old when he bombed Zeppelin LZ 37; he died in a flying accident just ten days later.

A postcard with an artist's rendition of Warneford's successful attack on Zeppelin LZ 37 over Ghent, Belgium, in the early hours of 7 June 1915.

The LZ 37 Memorial
Westerbegraafplaats (Western Cemetery) Ghent

Memorial to the crew of Zeppelin LZ 37

When Flight sub-Lieutenant Reginald Warneford destroyed Zeppelin LZ 37 over Ghent in the early hours of 7 June 1915, the fiercely burning wreck plummeted down and smashed into a convent in the St Amandsberg district of the city. Incredibly, one of the crew, Alfred Mühler, survived. He was thrown clear of the Zeppelin's front gondola and miraculously landed on a – vacated – nun's bed. The rest of the nine-man crew, however, all died.

Initially the crew were buried in Ghent's Westerbegraafplaats (Western Cemetery), although a month later one man – Wilhelm Müller – was exhumed by request of his family, taken back to Germany and reinterred in Bonn. The other seven men (the officers, Oberleutnant Otto van der Haegen and Oberleutnant Kurt Ackermann, and five crewmen, Carl Claus, Hermann Kirchner, Karl Mahr, Gustav Ruske and Otto Schwarz) remained in Ghent. Shortly afterwards, the wealthy Ackermann family secured a piece of land 10 metres square at the cemetery on which the German authorities built an impressive monument, designed by Professor Wilhelm Kreis, to honour of the loss of LZ 37 and her crew. The inauguration of the monument took place in January 1917 and three years later, by relocating other German bodies in the cemetery to surround it, the monument became the centrepiece of a German sector. At some point paving slabs were added around the monument. In 1956 the Volksbund Deutsche Kriegsgräberfürsorge (German War Graves Commission) or VDK, began a process of collecting up bodies from smaller cemeteries and bringing them together at larger centres. At this time they moved LZ 37's five crewmen to the military cemetery at Vladslo in Belgium. For many years, however, a mystery remained as to what happened to van der Haegen and Ackermann as they do not appear in the VDK records alongside the other five men.

Thanks to the efforts of local historians we now have an answer. When the VDK exhumed the other bodies, those of van der Haegen and Ackermann were in the ground acquired by Ackermann's family and therefore considered to be in private graves, not military, and were left. Those historians now believe that van der Haegen and Ackermann lie under the paving directly in front of the monument, on which is inscribed their names.

The impressive memorial to Zeppelin LZ 37 and her crew, unveiled in January 1917. LZ 37 had crashed in flames at Ghent after an attack by a British pilot. The paving stone in the foreground is believed to mark where the body of Oberleutnant Otto van der Haegen lies buried.

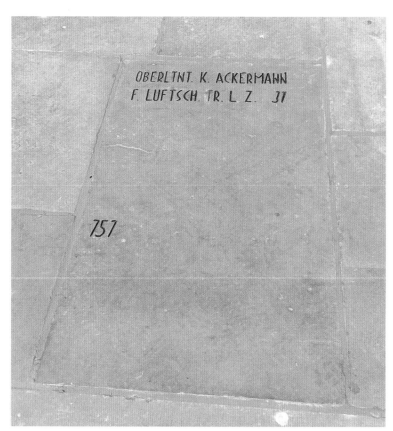

OBERLTNT. K. ACKERMANN
F. LUFTSCH. TR. L. Z. 37

757

LEFT: The paving slab marking the grave of Oberleutnant Kurt Ackermann lies to the right front of the memorial. Research by local historians has resulted in the identification of the graves of Ackermann and van der Haegen.

BELOW: LZ 37 was an 'm-class' Zeppelin. She first flew in February 1915 but was destroyed in an attack by British pilot Reginald Warneford just over three months later as she was returning from an aborted raid on England.

16

Zeplo

A board game of the First Blitz

The news of 'Rex' Warneford's success against Zeppelin LZ 37 in June 1915 went someway to breaking the aura of invincibility that had grown up around the Zeppelins, an achievement widely celebrated back in Britain. If you were a commercial organisation, why not try to make this story work for you? This example may have been one of the earliest attempts to capitalise on the destruction of a Zeppelin – the board game Zeplo.

Although the publication date is unknown, the picture on one side shows a monoplane dropping a bomb on a Zeppelin, reminiscent of Warneford's attack. However, the image of a damaged Zeppelin in the sea on one of the penalty squares is rather similar to images of Zeppelin L15 brought down on 31 March 1916. The game was in fact a marketing ploy by the London & Provincial Furnishing Co. of Norwich, described as 'A contest between British

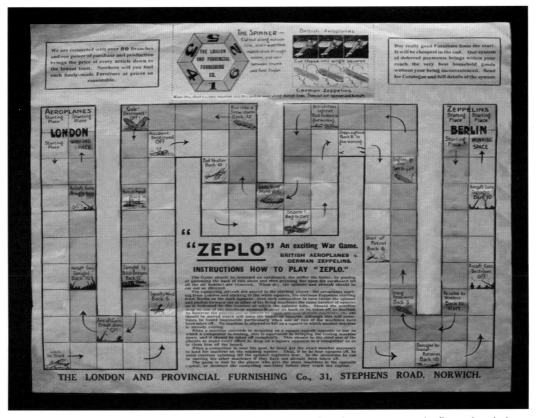

The game of Zeplo – 'an exciting war game' – in which the opposing players attempt to be first to bomb the enemy's capital. (The David Marks Collection)

aeroplanes and German Zepps', and explains that, 'This game is most exciting, and well worth playing and keeping'. Around the central picture the furniture company displayed various items from their stock while claiming, 'Nowhere will you find such finely-made Furniture at prices so reasonable'.

On the reverse of the paper sheet is the game board, with playing pieces to cut out and a spinner to use in place of a dice. The aim of the game is to get your aircraft to the opposing player's capital; the British player has three aeroplanes and the German three Zeppelins. Each player flies their aircraft on a separate path along which they may encounter a number of hazards. Engine trouble, bad weather or damage by AA guns can send the British player backwards, while flying accidents or heavier AA fire can destroy their aeroplanes. For the German player, the negatives include a wireless recall, strong winds, engine problems and attacks by Naval patrols, while strong gales or AA gunfire could destroy a Zeppelin on the way to London. Both players face an additional danger; if you can ensure your playing piece lands opposite an enemy piece, it will immediately lead to the destruction of your opponent's piece. Victory is achieved by getting more playing pieces to the enemy capital than your opponent – or by destroying all three of his aircraft. Considering the time, the designer had a good awareness of the problems involved in launching air raids and it is harder than it looks to battle your way through all the obstacles and make it all the way to the enemy capital in one piece!

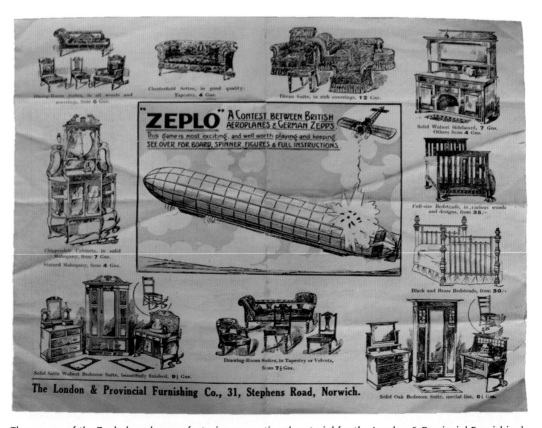

The reverse of the Zeplo board game, featuring promotional material for the London & Provincial Furnishing's range of furniture. (The David Marks Collection)

17

Palmer's Shipbuilding & Iron Company Plaque, Jarrow, County Durham

An air raid on the industrial north-east

On the night of 15 June 1915, Zeppelin L 10 appeared over north-east England and made a damaging bombing run over the industrial complexes lining the banks of the River Tyne. A number of bombs struck Palmer's Shipbuilding & Iron Company at Jarrow, where the night shift was in full production. They had not received warning of a raid and as such all the lights were blazing, making it an ideal target. Most damage occurred at the engine works and the erecting shop, where the blast of the bombs shattered the glass roofs, sending lethal shards of jagged glass flying among the workers below. The bombs at Palmer's killed 16 and injured another 72.

In 1920 the management erected a brass plaque in memory of the men killed in the raid. For unexplained reasons the plaque names only 12 of the 16 killed. The four not on the plaque are Joseph Lane, Joseph Thornicroft, Frederick Pinnock and William Stamford. Philip Strong, a genealogist researcher related to Joseph Lane, believes it possible that as Lane and Thornicroft were engineers they may not have been direct employees of Palmer's. That does not, however, explain the inclusion of William Young and

The original Palmer's plaque commemorating 12 of the 16 killed at the shipyard during the raid by Zeppelin L 10 in June 1915. (Courtesy of North-East War Memorials Project (NEWMP))

N HONOUR OF

ALBERT BRAMLEY
MATTHEW CARTER
JOHN CUTHBERT DAVISON
KARL KALNIN
ROBERT THOMAS NIXON
LAWRENCE FRAZER SANDERSON

THOMAS HENRY SMITH
RALPH SNAITH
WILLIAM GRIEVES TURNER
GEORGE WARD
JOHN GEORGE WINDLE
WILLIAM ERSKINE COOK YOUNG

WHO WERE KILLED NEAR THIS SPOT BY A BOMB DROPPED FROM A GERMAN AIRSHIP WHILST ERVING THEIR KING AND COUNTRY ON THE NIGHT OF 15 JUNE 1915 · THIS MEMORIAL ERECTED BY THE BOARD OF DIRECTORS OF PALMERS.

Lawrence Sanderson on the plaque. Both aged 16, it appears neither worked for Palmer's, but were present as they were bringing in food for others working the night shift. Frederick Pinnock, one of those not named on the plaque, was working at the soaking pit at Palmer's steelworks. This might be a clue; the plaque says that the 12 'were killed near this spot', perhaps the others were simply elsewhere within the complex at the time they were killed.

The plaque itself has been an item of interest down the years. In the late 1930s Sterling Foundry Specialities Ltd took over Palmer's and when, in the late 1960s, the company moved to new premises in Ellison Road, Jarrow, they took the plaque with them. But in the late '70s, Sterling closed down and Vince Rea, the owner of the Bede Gallery in Jarrow, acquired the plaque. The gallery itself closed down in 1996 and the plaque disappeared before resurfacing in December 2015 at an auction of the gallery's collection. This historic plaque is now in the collection of the South Shields Museum and Art Gallery.[18]

An artist's impression of Palmer's Shipbuilding and Iron Works at Jarrow on the banks of the River Tyne.

18

Air Raid Insurance

Protecting your home from air attack

One of the new developments following the first air raids was the introduction of air raid insurance. It appears some insurers had already developed policies prior to the first air raids as just two days after the first Zeppelin attack on East Anglia, the British Dominions General Insurance Company took out an advert in the *Daily Telegraph* promoting their comprehensive policy offering compensation for damage and loss caused by 'Zeppelins-Aircraft-Bombs-Shot-Shell-Bombardment-Invasion-Explosions-Fire-Riots-Strikes-Civil Commotion-Burglary'. The advert also advised readers that ordinary fire policies did not cover 'damage by fire from acts of war'. The premium paid depended on where you lived. In London the cost was 20s per £100 covered, on the south coast it was 25s, on the

An insurance leaflet issued by the *Daily News* offering a payment of £250 to householders 'in the case of damage by aerial attack', or a payment of £25 for damage caused by 'bombardment from the sea, or by our own anti-aircraft guns' – but only to those who subscribed to the newspaper.

SUN INSURANCE OFFICE.

Agency

Head Office: THREADNEEDLE STREET, LONDON, E.C.

ACTING AS AN AGENT FOR HIS MAJESTY'S GOVERNMENT.

Proposal for Insurance

— AGAINST —

AIR-CRAFT AND BOMBARDMENT RISKS

Under the Government Scheme.

PROPOSER'S NAME (in full)

(If Lady, please state whether Mrs. or Miss)

RESIDENCE

PROFESSION OR TRADE

IS LOSS ARISING FROM BOMBARDMENT AS WELL
AS THAT BY AIR-CRAFT TO BE COVERED ?

N.B.—Air-Craft Loss only may be covered, but not Bombardment Loss apart from Air-Craft Loss. Bombardment Risk will be
limited to " Bombardment by hostile guns not landed on British Territory."

On property as described in Fire Policy No.   with the   £
SUN INSURANCE OFFICE, and for the sum or sums expressed therein   ...   .

*If the Property is covered against damage by Fire with a Company not acting
as an approved Company under the Scheme, please state the name of such
Company, the No. of Policy, and particulars of the Insurance. If the Property
is not at present insured against loss by Fire, details should be supplied
and the amount or amounts to be insured stated, and such Insurance will be
subject to average.*

On property as follows (state situation and how occupied, and give separate valuations on
each distinct building and the contents of each and on Rent) :—

£

Rates per cent. per annum :—	Air-Craft only.		Air-Craft and Bombardment.	
	s.	d.	s.	d.
1. Building, Rent and Contents of Private Dwelling-houses and Buildings in which no trade or manufacture is carried on ...	2	0	3	0
2. All other Buildings and their Rents	3	0	4	6
3. Farming Stocks (live and dead)	3	0	4	6
4. Contents of all Buildings other than those specified in 1 and 5	5	0	7	0
5. (a) Merchandise at Docks and Public Wharves, in Carriers' and Canal Warehouses and Yards, in Public Mercantile Storage Warehouses, and in transit by Rail (b) Timber in the open ... ... (c) Mineral Oil Tanks and Stores (Wholesale)	7	6	10	0

No cover can be given until the premium required has been paid.
This proposal form is issued by the SUN INSURANCE OFFICE, as an Agent for His Majesty's
Government.

Proposer's Signature   *Date*

An insurance proposal form for 'Aircraft and Bombardment Risks' under the Government scheme introduced in July 1915. (The David Marks Collection)

east coast 40s, but elsewhere the premium was just 10s per £100. Many newspapers, seeing a marketing opportunity, arranged deals with insurance companies to offer their readers free insurance; the *Daily News* offered a payment of £250 'in the case of damage by aerial attack' and £25 'in the case of damage by bombardment from the sea, or by our own anti-aircraft guns'. At the same time the Government was accepting appeals for 'relief' from individuals who had been directly affected by air raids.

Amid mounting pressure on the Government to provide a national air raid insurance scheme, on 13 July 1915 such a scheme was announced in Parliament.[19] The scheme would involve existing fire insurance companies acting as agents for the Government 'in the issuing of policies and the collection of premiums, and in the initial proceedings in connection with loss adjustments'. The policies would cover loss and damage to the property insured caused directly or indirectly by aircraft or bombardment. For

County Fire Office, Limited.

APPOINTED TO ACT AS AGENT FOR THE

GOVERNMENT SCHEME OF

AIRCRAFT & BOMBARDMENT INSURANCE

Policy No.	NAME OF INSURED.	Amount Insured.	Premium Payable.
		£	£ s. d.
108844.	C. H. Jackson	200 Less 50 per cent. Discount ...	4 . . 2 .

Premium Payable £ : 2 : .

AGENCY: 252, KENNINGTON RD LONDON, S.E.//

191

SIR OR MADAM,

We beg to inform you that your Policy as above will expire on the *30th Sept* . 191 *7*, and, if it is desired to continue the Insurance thereunder, the Premium should be paid to me at the above address on or before that date.

If the property insured is now ratable in a different class from that in which it was rated at the time the original Policy was effected, the Insured must notify the Office and pay the appropriate Premium. The removal of property from a private house to premises occupied for Trade purposes, or to a Furniture Depository, would bring the Insurance under a higher rated class. (For list of Classes see overleaf).

It is important that this Notice should be produced or the Policy Number quoted when the Premium is paid.

Yours faithfully,

C H White

AGENT.

N.B.—Your special attention is drawn to the fact that no days of grace for the renewal of a Policy are allowed under the Government Scheme.

5

An insurance renewal advice sent to C. H. Jackson advising him that his cover was due to end on 30 September 1917. Hopefully Mr Jackson renewed as that date coincided with the 'Harvest Moon Offensive', the most concentrated period of bombing on London during the war. (The David Marks Collection)

a private household the cost would be 2s per annum for insurance against damage by aircraft, or 3s per annum against aircraft and bombardment damage. In November 1915 the Government announced another scheme, specifically aimed at 'working class property'. For property worth less than £100, insurance could be bought over the counter at the Post Office at a cost of 6d per annum for insurance of £25, while 1s bought cover of £50 and 1s 6d provided insurance of £75.[20]

Later in the war, in November 1917, the Government announced free compensation for damage caused by aerial attack of up to £500.[21]

19

Zeppelin Raid Memorial
Goole, East Yorkshire
Commemorating civilian casualties

On the night of 9 August 1915, Kapitänleutnant Odo Loewe, commanding a Zeppelin over Britain for the first time, brought L 9 inland looking for Hull. A thick mist, however, hindered his navigation, as did a broken rudder cable. When Loewe finally saw lights he thought he had found his target, but in fact he was approaching Goole, 22 miles further inland. Loewe released five incendiary bombs outside the town, then eight high-explosive bombs and 13 incendiaries over the town, with 16 more incendiaries dropping near the railway and docks. The bombs on the town claimed 16 killed and 11 injured.

After the raid, the bodies of the victims were buried together in six graves dug in a circular plot in Goole Cemetery. Following the end of the conflict, a War Memorial Committee formed to consider how best to commemorate Goole's fallen. In January 1919 a vote approved various proposals, including a war memorial and three parks. In addition, the committee voted for a memorial to the victims of the Zeppelin raid on

The names of the victims of the Goole Zeppelin laid out on a marble page of an open book, part of the raid memorial in Goole cemetery. (Courtesy of the Goole First World War Research Group)

the town, raising funds by public subscription. After encountering a number of difficulties, only a war memorial, a garden and the Zeppelin raid memorial were created. The raid memorial, erected over the victims' graves, was unveiled in February 1922 with 5,000 people in attendance.[22]

Crafted by a well-respected local monumental mason, H. O. Tasker, the memorial features an open book carved from marble bearing an inscription and the names and ages of the victims in lead letters.

Over the years the memorial suffered from weathering and some lettering became difficult to read, but in July 2015, guided by the Goole First World War Research Group, the town council began restoration work. The surface of the memorial was ground back and new lettering applied ensuring all names were legible once more in time for the centenary of the raid in August 2015.

There are few memorials erected solely to commemorate civilian air raid casualties of the First World War, which makes the fact that the Goole memorial is now in such good condition something of which the community should be rightly proud. The restored memorial now has Grade II listed status for reasons of Historical Interest, Design Interest and Rarity.

The beautifully restored Zeppelin raid memorial; work was completed in time for the centenary in 2015. (Courtesy of the Goole First World War Research Group)

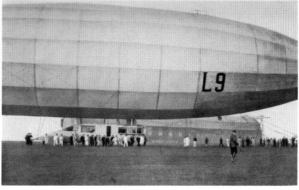

Zeppelin L 9, commanded by Odo Loewe, which carried out the attack on Goole on the night of 9 August 1915.

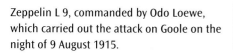

20

3-inch 20 cwt Anti-Aircraft Gun
Dover, Kent

The first British AA gun to cripple a Zeppelin

Shortly after midnight on 10 August 1915, Zeppelin L 12, commanded by Oberleutnant-zur-See Werner Peterson, approached the well-defended port of Dover. As searchlights opened on L 12, so did the Dover guns. From Langdon Fort (also known as Langdon Battery) a 3-inch 20 cwt gun and two 1-pdr 'pom-poms' commenced firing, joined by two 6-pdrs from the Drop Redoubt and three 'pom-poms' based at Dover Castle. With L 12 flying at only 5,000 feet, Peterson dropped bombs and water ballast to climb out of range as quickly as possible but the second or third round fired by the 3-inch gun hit home and ripped open two of the 16 gas cells. Although the shell did not ignite the hydrogen, its loss meant the craft was in trouble. Attempting to get back home, L 12 gradually lost height and came down in the sea.

The restored 3-inch 20 cwt anti-aircraft gun on display at Dover Castle, Kent. (Courtesy of Michael Garlick; www.geograph.org.uk)

The crew spent an anxious night huddled on the top of the floundering airship until a German Navy destroyer appeared and towed it into the harbour at Ostend. The 3-inch 20 cwt AA gun at Dover was the first British gun to have crippled a Zeppelin. Later that day L 12's fate was sealed when fire broke out during the salvage operation and destroyed it.

At the beginning of the war Britain had six 3-inch guns allocated to aerial defence, which increased to 19 by November 1915. These guns proved the most effective of the Home Defence guns, and in June 1918, of the 469 guns of five types employed by the Army for air defence, 255 were 3-inch 20 cwt. At the same time, the Navy had 25 AA guns, of which all but two were 3-inch.

Although the 3-inch 20 cwt gun was the most numerous of the Home Defence AA guns, there are now but a handful left in museums and collections. In 1994 English Heritage acquired one from the Ministry of Defence. Having based it at Pendennis Castle in Cornwall, restoration work commenced later to return the gun back to full working order, and it is now the only one in the world capable of being fired. In 2015 the gun moved from Cornwall to Dover Castle in Kent, where it now forms part of a recreated anti-aircraft gun position, its installation completed in time for the centenary of the Dover gun's success against Zeppelin L 12.

RIGHT: Following damage inflicted by a shell fired from a 3-inch 20 cwt anti-aircraft gun at Dover, Zeppelin L 12 is towed into Ostend harbour by a German destroyer. (The David Marks Collection)

BELOW: The remains of L 12 in Ostend harbour after a fire broke out and destroyed the already damaged Zeppelin.

21

Woodbridge Postcards

A series of postcards revealing the impact
of Zeppelin bombs on a Suffolk town

On 12 August 1915, three of the four Zeppelins that set out to attack England turned back early with mechanical problems. The remaining Zeppelin, Oberleutnant-zur-See Friedrich Wenke's L 10, intended to strike against London but her commander switched to the secondary target of Harwich after encountering strong headwinds. Crossing the Suffolk coast and heading south, he approached the town of Woodbridge, where men of the 2/3rd London Brigade were stationed.

Seeing the looming Zeppelin overhead, soldiers opened up with a machine gun and rifle fire, which Wenke responded to by dropping four high-explosive (HE) and 20 incendiary bombs.

The most damaging and destructive of these was the HE bomb that exploded on the pavement outside No. 1 St John's Hill. Unfortunately, the sound of the Army's gunfire had attracted residents to their doors and windows. The explosion shattered No. 1 but the family inside narrowly escaped without injury. However, inside

One of the series of Stephenson postcards showing bomb damage in St John's Hill. Those in the street are looking at No. 1, outside which the bomb exploded. (The David Marks Collection)

Zeppelin Raid on Woodbridge. August 12th. 1915. Pub by Stephenson Woodbridge

the house next door, on the corner of St John's Hill and New Street, 67-year-old Eliza Bunn suffered fatal injuries. Across the street, Mr and Mrs Tyler were standing in their doorway at No. 4 when the bomb exploded. The blast killed Mrs Tyler instantly and her husband died shortly afterwards, but their three young children in the house were untouched. The blast also killed two men in the street: Edward Turner, a volunteer fireman on his way to report for duty, and Dennis Harris. The final victim, 16-year-old James Marshall, was at home at No. 27 New Street. His family had just left the house to seek better shelter and he was going to join them as soon as he had drunk his cocoa. He never finished it.

An enterprising local printer and stationer, E. W. Stephenson, produced a set of six postcards showing the bomb damage around St John's Hill. The photographs graphically show the widespread effects of just one bomb. For those customers with a more morbid interest, two of the postcards are marked with an 'x': one shows where Mr and Mrs Tyler were standing when they were killed and the other the shattered entrance to the room in which the dying Eliza Bunn had been found. These marks make this set of bomb damage postcards unique among those produced during the war. The postcard that marks the Tylers' house also shows the tarpaulin-covered house in New Street where James Marshall died.

Another of Stephenson's postcards, this one indicating No. 4 St John's Hill with an 'X', where Mr and Mrs Tyler were standing watching the raid when the bomb exploded and killed them both. (The David Marks Collection)

This postcard marks the home of Eliza Bunn in St John's Hill with an 'X'; here she was killed by the bomb. A group of four civilians are surveying the destruction while a women strides purposefully through the rubble. (The David Marks Collection)

22

German Commemorative Medallion

Struck to mark the first raid on London by a German Navy Zeppelin

In Germany, commemorative medallions were a highly popular art form. During the war they were used to illustrate a wide range of subjects, including military and political leaders, propaganda, satirical observations on the war, military victories and, of course, Zeppelins.

On the night of 17 August 1915, Zeppelin L 10, commanded by Oberleutnant-zur-See Friedrich Wenke, became the first Navy Zeppelin to bomb London. In his detailed report Wenke stated:

'Since it had turned into a clear, starry night, I steered for the west end of the city, in order to have the wind abaft the beam. At 11.30pm [10.30pm British time] I turned to an easterly course and crossed the centre of the city at 3,100 metres, a little north of the Thames. Bomb dropping was ordered to begin between Blackfriars and London Bridges. Collapse of buildings and big fires could be observed.'[23]

Unusually for Wenke, his navigation was off course that night. British reports, in fact, state the sky was cloudy, and it appears from his position two miles high that he mistook glimpses of the great line of reservoirs running down the Lea Valley for the Thames. Rather than striking near the Thames, all his bombs fell between Walthamstow and the open space of Wanstead Flats, via Leyton and Leytonstone.

A large version of the 'Luftangriff auf London' medallion on display at the Zeppelin Museum in Friedrichshafen in Germany.

A copy of the original artist's impression of Zeppelin L 10's raid on London in August 1915, which inspired the image used on the medallion. The artwork itself was based on the report of the raid submitted by the commander of L 10, Friedrich Wenke.

Following Wenke's raid, his report became public in Germany and an artist quickly produced a dramatic rendition of his action over London, showing L 10 looming over Tower Bridge as shells explode around her. On 15 September the popular British weekly publication, *The Illustrated War News*, reproduced it the image in their pages with the bristling editorial comment that it was 'bombastically inaccurate'.

In Germany, medallist Friedrich 'Fritz' Eue clearly used the illustration as inspiration for a large medallion, just over 10cm in diameter, entitled 'Luftangriff auf London (Air raid on London) 17.18.8.1915'. The only difference between the original illustration and that reproduced on the reverse of the medallion is the addition of a second Zeppelin in the distance. The obverse shows a bust of Count Zeppelin. Although mostly manufactured in iron, the example in the Zeppelin Museum, Friedrichshafen, Germany, appears to be made of bronze. A smaller version measuring 34mm in diameter was also produced in silver.

23

'In Memoriam' Cards

Remembering the dead

During the Victorian era, when mourning the death of family and friends had become a highly ritualised process, one of the many items associated with it were 'In Memoriam' cards.

The advent of aerial bombing in the First World War brought death to the streets of Britain and from the mounting numbers of civilian casualties, many of them children, there emerged a shared experience of loss. For those unconnected to the families, 'In Memoriam' cards were a chance to express their grief for the loss of others. These cards, edged in black and silver, generally gave the date of the air raid and offered a short poem or prayer. They were printed quickly and made available soon after the air raids, often before the names of the victims were known. These examples measure nine inches by three inches, but were folded in half.

The earliest example shown here is 'In loving memory of the poor victims' of the August 1915 Zeppelin raid on London, when ten people died. The same design was used for the September 1915 raids on London. It is not clear whether this card relates to one or two raids as there was a raid either side of midnight on the night of 7/8 September and another on the night of 8 September. Commemorating both raids in a single card would make economic sense as there were 40 people killed in the two raids. These two cards from 1915 use the same poem. Two later cards, from raids in 1917, share a different poem.

The printer of these cards is S. Burgess, who worked from 8 York Place, off the Strand in London. She was a prolific and versatile printer, well known for commemorative ephemera, particularly printed napkins. She imported the flimsy paper squares with printed borders from Japan and overprinted with a commemorative message in England (see Object 77). Burgess

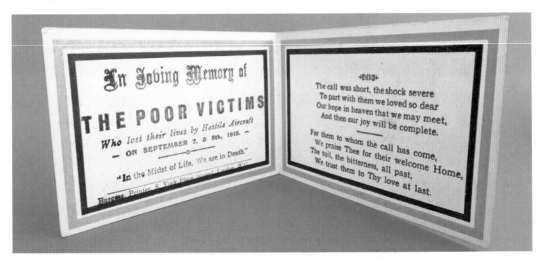

A memoriam card commemorating the victims of Zeppelin raids on London in September 1915.

produced commemorative napkins in support of women's suffrage in 1908 and 1909, and in 1912 printed one to mark the sinking of the *Titanic*. The company also printed and published a spoof newspaper based on the *Daily Mail*, called the *Daily Liar*. All the cards shown here are printed by Burgess, which dominated the market in London and the South-east.

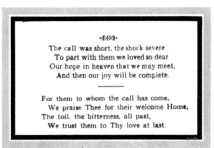

The earliest 'In memoriam' card that I have seen so far, commemorating the victims of the second Zeppelin raid on London, which took place on the night of 17 August 1915. Bombs killed ten people that night. (The David Marks Collection)

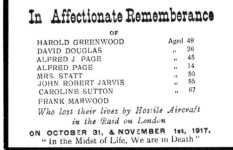

This card is in memory of the victims of the Gotha raid on the night of 31 October/1 November 1917 and incorporates an image of a Boy Scout in reference to 14-year-old Alfred Page. Alfred was on duty that night, waiting to go out and sound the 'all clear' on his bugle when the bomb that killed him also killed his father and destroyed the family home. (The David Marks Collection)

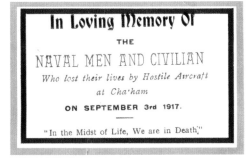

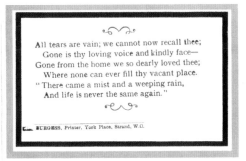

Another 1917 card, this one commemorating those killed in the Gotha raid on the Chatham naval barracks on 3 September (See Object 85). This card uses the same poem as that featured on the 31 October card. (The David Marks Collection)

24

Queen Square Bomb Plaque
Bloomsbury, London
A miraculous escape from injury

On 8 September 1915, Kapitänleutnant Heinrich Mathy, commanding Zeppelin L 13, carried out a raid on central London that shocked the capital. The raid caused damage estimated at £530,787 (at 1915 costs), the most inflicted by any raid in the war, killing 22 people and injuring another 87. Yet the total could have been significantly higher.

The first high-explosive bomb dropped on central London exploded in Queen Square, Bloomsbury, at about 10.45pm. Rather than being 'square', Queen Square was an elongated rectangular garden enclosed on all four sides by buildings that were home to hospitals, medical facilities and hotels.

John Stuart, an actor recovering from a minor operation, was in a hospital in Great Ormond Street, a road leading into Queen Square. He had just dropped off to sleep when he awoke. 'The Matron came into the ward and ordered all lights to be extinguished. Suddenly there was a terrific crash and a splintering of glass nearby.'[24]

The bomb landed towards the north end of the square, where it exploded, damaging a flower pedestal and a statue. The blast wave from the explosion struck the surrounding buildings. It

The discreet brass plaque in the centre of a paving circle in Queen Square. The wording on the plaque highlights the fortuitous escape from injury of those in the hospitals and hotels that surrounded the square.

smashed windows at the Alexandra Hospital for Children, the National Hospital for the Paralysed and Epileptic, the Examination Hall of the Royal College of Physicians and Surgeons, the Home for Working Boys, three hotels or boarding houses, and at the offices of the Art Workers' Guild. Despite the great number of vulnerable people close by, the effect of the bomb was limited, as was made clear when a commemorative plaque was installed in the square after the war.

The small plaque lies inconspicuously in the gardens in the shade of a tree, set in a circle of paving marking the spot where the bomb fell. The inscription bears the words:

'On the night of the eighth of September 1915 a Zeppelin bomb fell and exploded on this spot. Although nearly one thousand people slept in the surrounding buildings no person was injured.'

The square remains largely unchanged from the time of the raid, with many of the buildings surrounding the gardens occupied by hospital departments and with the Art Workers' Guild still located at 6 Queen Square.

The paving circle in Queen Square, London, marking where the first high-explosive bomb fell during Heinrich Mathy's 8 September 1915 raid on London.

25

The Dolphin Tavern's Clock
Holborn, London

A pub smashed by a bomb's blast

On the night of 8 September 1915, just minutes after Kapitänleutnant Heinrich Mathy released the high-explosive bomb over Queen Square, another hurtled down as Zeppelin L 13 passed over Theobald's Road, Holborn. Running south from Theobald's Road is Red Lion Street and standing at the junction of these two roads was a branch of the National Penny Bank. Directly behind the bank stood The Dolphin Tavern, on the corner of Lamb's Conduit Passage, a narrow thoroughfare running off Red Lion Street. Between the tavern and the bank stood a single gas lamp.

Henry Coombs, a 23-year-old stable hand, had just emerged from The Dolphin and was waiting at the entrance for a friend who had gone to a fried fish shop in the passage, when a high-explosive bomb struck the gas lamp and detonated no more than six feet from where he stood. The bomb ripped up a twelve feet by ten feet section of the paving, flinging great lumps of stone through the air, smashing the gas main

The Dolphin Tavern clock, recovered from the wreckage of the pub. Although the explosion broke the clock's mechanism, it remains in place, a survivor of the First Blitz.

below, gutting the ground floor of the bank and destroying the frontage of the pub. Coombs died instantly. The same bomb also caused substantial damage to The Enterprise, a pub directly opposite on Red Lion Street. Serious fires broke out in Lamb's Conduit Passage, where 16 people were injured and a fireman, John Samuel Green, later died of his terrible burns.

When salvage teams sifted through the rubble, splintered wood and shattered glass of The Dolphin, they found a clock. The clock was broken, stopped at 10.49pm, the moment the bomb exploded. Later, after the pub's restoration, the clock was reinstated, its hands frozen in time. The clock is still there today. Although its minute hand has 'dropped' nine minutes over the intervening century, and its face has yellowed with age, this unique clock provides a tangible link to a shocking night in London's history. Across the road, The Enterprise is also still open for business, while the building occupied by the Penny Bank is now a betting shop, but the upper storeys remain as they were in 1915.

An extraordinarily detailed scale model showing the damage caused by the bomb is in storage at the Museum of London, although the original purpose of the model is unclear.

An extraordinarily detailed model showing the bomb damage inflicted on The Dolphin Tavern and the National Penny Bank. At one time at the Imperial War Museum, the model is now in the collection of the Museum of London. (Courtesy of the Museum of London)

A close-up view of the bomb damage inflicted on The Dolphin Tavern and National Penny Bank as shown on the model in the collection of the Museum of London. Henry Coombs was killed standing at the entrance to the pub, which was obliterated by the bomb. (Courtesy of the Museum of London)

26

Farringdon Road Plaque
Clerkenwell, London

A symbol of destruction and restoration

As Heinrich Mathy continued on his path of destruction across central London on 8 September 1915, a bomb he dropped in Farringdon Road has given us arguably the most well-known plaque in London associated with the First Blitz. It regularly appears on websites, in blogs, books and in television documentaries, but what is the story behind it?

Having begun his bombing run over Bloomsbury, Mathy dropped more bombs over Holborn, Gray's Inn and Hatton Garden, before passing down Farringdon Road, which ran alongside the Metropolitan Railway. The west side of Farringdon Road was developed commercially in the late 1880s and the section from Nos. 47 to 73 was designed by architects William Dunk and John Mease Geden as terraced warehouses, each being six storeys high with just a narrow frontage onto the street.

A high-explosive bomb dropped from Zeppelin L 13 struck No. 61, where the main occupiers were the Brass Foundry & Lamp Co. Ltd., who used the premises as a showroom, office and store. The explosion of the bomb destroyed the roof and severely damaged the upper three floors along with their contents. The other floors

The plaque on the front of No. 61 Farringdon Road, London. It is perhaps one of the best known of the London plaques associated with the First Blitz. (Historic Military Press)

THESE PREMISES
WERE TOTALLY DESTROYED
BY A
ZEPPELIN RAID
DURING THE WORLD WAR
ON
SEPTEMBER 8TH 1915
REBUILT 1917

JOHN PHILLIPS
GOVERNING DIRECTOR

were damaged by fire, smoke and water. Falling masonry from the building also damaged the drill hall of the 6th (City of London) Battalion of The London Regiment (City of London Rifles), located behind the warehouse. The premises on either side, No. 59, occupied by gas engineers, J. Milne & Sons, and No. 63, home to telescope manufacturers Broadhurst, Clarkson & Co., both suffered damage, while many other premises in the street experienced broken windows. However, it was No. 61 that bore the brunt of the explosion.[25]

In fact, the building was in such a bad condition that inspectors considered it beyond repair and took the decision to rebuild it. The new building, completed to the same design, reopened just two years later. A plaque placed close to the pavement on the front of No. 61 commemorates the destruction of the building by the Zeppelin bomb and its subsequent rebuilding.

Over the years Nos. 59 and 61 Farringdon Road have merged and are now known as the Zeppelin Building, while high up on No. 63 a sign bearing the name Telescope House serves as a reminder of the original occupants, the company continuing trading there until 2006.

The frontage of Nos. 59–61 Farringdon Road, now known as the Zeppelin Building, with the entrance to the Drill Hall on the left. (Historic Military Press).

Through an archway to the left of Nos. 59–61 Farringdon Road is the old drill hall of the 6th (City of London) Battalion of The London Regiment, which also suffered damage from the bomb.

27

The Wrotham Park Bone – Hertfordshire

German humour of the First Blitz

Heinrich Mathy's raid over London in L 13 on 8 September was the most damaging Zeppelin attack of the war. The British authorities traced 15 high-explosive bombs and 55 incendiaries dropped during his passage over the capital – and, curiously, one more object that lacked any deadly intent. This unusual item reflected rather more on the sense of humour of an unknown member of the crew.

The Zeppelin came inland over The Wash, passed over Cambridgeshire and Hertfordshire, before reaching Potter's Bar at 10.28pm. Four minutes later observers noted seeing it over Barnet. Between these two places stands a magnificent country house and estate – Wrotham Park. Originally built in the mid-18th century for Admiral John Byng, despite destruction by fire in 1883, the house remains the home of the Byng family to this day after complete reconstruction in the original style.

As L 13 passed over Potter's Bar, someone on board threw out an animal bone attached to a small parachute. The parachute landed in the grounds of Wrotham Park, near the Bentley Heath Lodge entrance to the estate; after its discovery the Byng family handed it over to the authorities. Brief details of this unusual item appeared in the Press on 14 September.[26] The bone, a scapula (shoulder blade) of either a cow or horse (although incorrectly described later in a report by the Intelligence Section, General

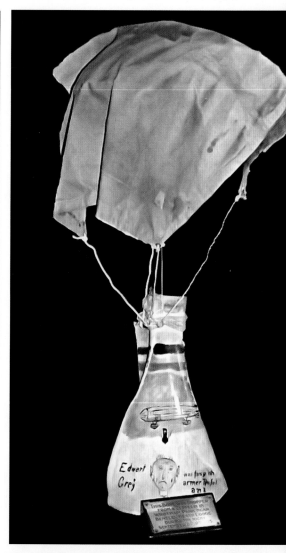

The animal bone dropped by parachute over Wrotham Park from Zeppelin L 13 as it prepared to make an attack on London on 8 September 1915. (With kind permission from the Wrotham Park Estate)

Headquarters, Home Forces, as a 'ham-bone'), bore an inscription and cartoon. With reference to the British naval blockade of German ports, the inscription reads, '*Zum Andenken an das ausgehungerte Deutschland*' (A memento from starved-out Germany). On the other side an image showed a crude depiction of a worried-looking Sir Edward Grey, the Foreign Secretary, with a Zeppelin bomb about to drop on his head. Alongside the drawing were the words '*Was fang ich, armer Teufel, an?*' (What shall I, poor devil, do?).

The Byng family later asked for the return of the bone and the Government obliged. This remarkable relic of the First Blitz remains with the family and, besides some necessary restoration to the parachute, the bone is in as good a condition as the day an unknown crewman of Zeppelin L 13 thought he would have some fun and dropped it over the side.

A close up of the front of the bone showing a cartoon of a Zeppelin dropping a bomb on the head of a rather worried-looking Sir Edward Grey. (With kind permission from the Wrotham Park Estate)

A view of the rear of the bone bearing the words, 'A memento from starved-out Germany'. (With kind permission from the Wrotham Park Estate)

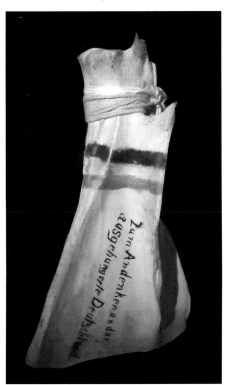

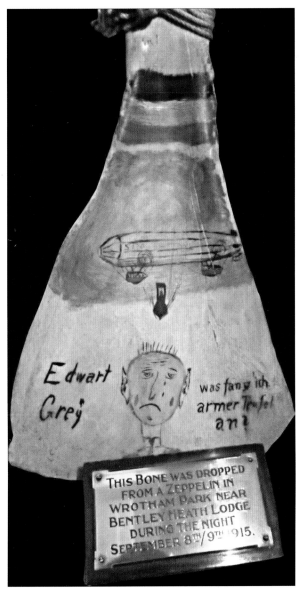

28

The Gateway of St Bartholomew-the-Great West Smithfield, London

A remarkable Tudor building revealed by a Zeppelin bomb

During his raid on London in Zeppelin L 13 on the night of 8 September 1915, Heinrich Mathy carried a 300kg high-explosive bomb, the heaviest so far dropped on London. The factory that built the bomb sent it as a *Liebesgabe* – a 'gift of love' – for the airship. Mathy released the bomb as he approached Smithfield Market; it struck the ground a little to the south of the market, exploding in the enclosed area of Bartholomew Close.

The impact of the bomb was catastrophic, with hardly a building left untouched by the blast. Mathy, looking down, was impressed. 'The explosive effect of the 300kg bomb,' he noted, 'must be very great, since a whole cluster of lights vanished in its crater.'[27] But its effect extended beyond the limits of the close, with the shockwave reaching over 100 yards in all directions. At St Bartholomew's

The timber-framed frontage of the gateway of the Church of St Bartholomew-the-Great in West Smithfield, London, revealed after the explosion of a 300kg high-explosive bomb in Bartholomew Close on 8 September 1915.

(St Barts) Hospital, where many of those injured in the raid received treatment, the blast smashed an estimated 1,200 windows. Although the historic priory church of St Bartholomew-the-Great escaped any injury, the bomb blast had a dramatic effect on its ancient gateway on West Smithfield. Part of the church, demolished in 1543 during Henry VIII's dissolution of the monasteries, was never rebuilt and the Norman arch that had previously formed the west entrance to the nave now served as the gateway to the churchyard. In 1595 a simple two-storey timber-framed dwelling was built over the gateway arch, but at some point during the 18th century Georgian tastes saw its frontage bricked over in the style of the day, leaving a very plain façade. Mathy's 300kg bomb changed all that.

The blast from the bomb shook many buildings in the surrounding area, and at the gateway many of the bricks fell away, exposing the original timber-framed frontage. Amazed by the discovery, the rector and churchwardens set about restoring the building, and it would seem they made a decent job of it as in August 1916 a journalist remarked on the 'beautiful oak and plaster façade which I had not noticed before'.[28] In 1932 the building underwent another restoration and is now a Grade II listed building, recognised as having one of the oldest timber-framed facades in London, all revealed as a consequence of Heinrich Mathy's *Liebesgabe*.

Shattered buildings in Bartholomew Close after the explosion of the 300kg bomb released by Heinrich Mathy's L 13. It was at the time the heaviest bomb dropped on Britain from the air and the shockwave caused damage over a wide area.

29

Hamerton's Grocery Shop
East Dereham, Norfolk

A nation of shopkeepers undaunted by German bombs

On 8 September 1915, while Zeppelin L 13 carried out the most damaging raid of the war on London, the commander of another raider, Kapitänleutnant-der-Reserve Alois Böcker, searched for the city of Norwich. When he felt Zeppelin L 14 was over the target he released 31 bombs; rather than striking Norwich, the bombs fell about 16 miles to the west, on the quiet market town of East Dereham. The reaction of the town's shopkeepers demonstrates a determination not to be bowed by the damage to their businesses.

Bombs in Church Street had a devastating effect, cutting down and killing a soldier, Lance Corporal Alfred Pomeroy, 2/1st City of London Yeomanry, and a jeweller, Henry Patterson. Ernest Tovell, a child at the time, later remembered, 'The bomb was outside Hamerton's shop. It took the front out and done a lot of damage. Also Mr Cave next door was also damaged.'[29]

The scales from R. Hamerton's grocery shop in East Dereham, Norfolk. The explosion of the bomb in Church Street blew in the front of the shop and damaged most of the stock, but the scales, an essential item in any grocery shop, survived. (Courtesy of Bishop Bonner's Cottage Museum)

Hamerton's was a grocery shop and Herbert Cave, a local photographer, had his glazed studio next door. A local newspaper reported: 'The whole front of Mr Hamerton's grocer's shop was blown out and his goods were scattered in the road. The entire place, indeed, was in ruins.'[30] And at Cave's studio not a single pane of glass survived intact.

Despite the impact the bombs had on their businesses, neither owner sat around moping. Although a bomb had wrecked his premises, Hamerton kept trading. Three days later a notice appeared in the local newspaper in which he apologised to his customers because for a short time he would be unable to give his 'customary prompt attention to orders'. It is clear that the bomb played havoc in the shop and to his home above it. The Bishop Bonner's Cottage Museum in Dereham holds a cup and plate donated by Hamerton's granddaughter, Nancy Briggs; they were the only pieces of the family's china to survive the bomb. From the chaos within the shop a set of scales survived.

Although the bomb caused extensive damage to his studio next door to Hamerton's, the following morning Cave was out with his camera recording the shocking moment in the town's history for posterity. No doubt selling copies of those photos as postcards allowed him to recover some of his losses. Like many other traders all over the country, both Hamerton and Cave displayed an early demonstration of the 'Blitz spirit', more commonly associated with the next war.

The blast of the bomb also caused serious damage to Hamerton's home above the shop. Many of the more fragile items were smashed but this cup and saucer survived and were recovered from the wreckage. (Courtesy of Bishop Bonner's Cottage Museum)

CHURCH STREET, EAST DEREHAM

DEAR MADAM OR SIR,—

Having been deprived of all facilities, for a short period I shall be unable to give the CUSTOMARY PROMPT ATTENTION TO ORDERS.

Difficult as it may be, I am anxious to RETAIN THE PATRONAGE I have enjoyed in the past, and beg your kind indulgence to the following extent:—

For the present, I shall only be able to be open for business from 10 to 1 and 2 till 6.

It would be esteemed a great favour if YOUR ORDERS could be BROUGHT OR SENT A DAY BEFORE GOODS ARE REQUIRED.

This also applies to Friends upon whom I have made regular calls, as I shall be UNABLE TO LEAVE THE PREMISES.

Assuring you of my best services, and of every effort to restore former conditions as soon as possible.

I am,

Yours respectfully,

R. HAMERTON.

The resilience of Britain's shopkeepers in the face of adversity is reflected in this advert taken out by Hamerton shortly after the raid. (Courtesy of Bishop Bonner's Cottage Museum)

A postcard showing Church Street, East Dereham, after the raid. The glass-fronted studio of H. T. Cave shows the effect of the bomb on its windows, while to the right, behind the lady wearing the white blouse, is the shattered frontage of Hamerton's grocery shop. (The David Marks Collection)

30

AA Gun Position on One Tree Hill
Honor Oak, London
Defending the capital

Towards the end of 1914, London's anti-aircraft gun defence had not grown significantly. The first three guns assigned to the capital's defence – 1pdr 'pom-poms' – appeared in August 1914. They were joined in the autumn by ten more guns (two 3-inch 20 cwt guns, three 6-pdrs and five 'pom-poms') all positioned in central London. It remained that way until a German aircraft flew up the Thames Estuary on Christmas Day 1914, reaching as far as Erith before a British aircraft engaged it, which persuaded the crew to turn back. Although prevented from reaching London, the threat stung the Government into

The 3-inch 20 cwt AA gun position on One Tree Hill at Honor Oak, London. The position was one of three forming an outer gun line to defend London, created in response to the flight up the River Thames by a German aeroplane on Christmas Day 1914.

action and, in response, it accepted a plan to establish a new ring of gun positions about six miles out from the centre of London. With a limited number of guns available, the decision led to the redirection of three 3-inch 20 cwt guns intended for the Fleet to the first sites selected for this new ring, at Parliament Hill, Clapton Orient Football Ground and at One Tree Hill, Honor Oak.[31] Of these three, the position on One Tree Hill in south-east London is still intact.

The raised platform on top of One Tree Hill, a commanding position overlooking the capital, built of brick and concrete by the Office of Works, provided a solid flat base for the gun. It is unclear when the position became operational but the gun first saw action on the night of 8 September 1915 when Heinrich Mathy's Zeppelin, L 13,

attacked the city. The gun opened fire at 10.51pm for nine minutes, during which time it fired 13 rounds.[32]

The gun was again in action on the night of 13 October 1915. At 9.35pm it opened on Zeppelin L 15, commanded by Kapitänleutnant Joachim Breithaupt, firing five rounds as it bombed central London in what became known as the 'Theatreland Raid'. Later, at 11.45pm, the gun engaged Heinrich Mathy's L 13 as it attacked Woolwich, firing nine more rounds.[33] The last mention of a gun on One Tree Hill was during the raid of 25/26 April 1916 but it did not come into action. It appears likely that at some point after this raid the gun moved to a new location as the gunnery defences continued to expand.

The brick platform of the gun position on One Tree Hill. The gun here first came into action during the Zeppelin raid on London of 8 September 1915.

31

Agnes Robins' Grave
Margate, Kent

The first person in Britain killed by an aeroplane bomb

Although many had anticipated that Germany would make its first aerial attack on Britain by Zeppelin, when that first raid did take place it was by aeroplane and not airship. After that first attack on 24 December 1914, individual and small-scale aeroplane and floatplane attacks continued spasmodically until they faded away once the Gotha bomber offensive commenced in May 1917. These early raids were not part of any great strategic plan and were generally of the 'hit-and-run' type. The first four raids only caused damage estimated at £70, without inflicting any casualties. The fifth raid, on 13 September 1915, however, produced a different result.

At 5.40pm a seaplane of *Seeflieger Abteilung 1* appeared in the sky over the Cliftonville district of Margate on the Kent coast. There had been no warning and those out enjoying a stroll presumed it to be British and looked on admiringly. Moments later, as a newspaper reported, that admiration turned to fear. 'When the hail of bombs suddenly descended, it was too late to seek shelter and many of the missiles fell upon the sands and cliff, in full view of those who were enjoying the September sunshine on the sea front.'[34]

Having dropped six bombs over the beach and cliff top area, the raiding aeroplane headed inland, dropping three more bombs along Godwin Road. The sound of explosions had

The Robins' family grave in St John's cemetery, Margate.

brought the inquisitive out into the street and as the next one detonated opposite No. 2 Godwin Road, flying fragments injured a woman standing at the door. A second bomb struck No. 14, injuring two ladies taking tea, followed by a third bomb that landed in a garden. Fragments from this bomb struck Agnes Robins outside the lodging house she ran at No. 26. Agnes, standing at her front door, had turned to go back inside when a bomb splinter smashed into her back, causing a serious puncture wound. The final bomb fell in Albion Road, injuring three people, one of them, Kate Bonny, seriously.

Both Agnes Robins (aged 40) and Kate Bonny (37) later succumbed to their wounds: Agnes died on 15 September, followed by Kate two days later. Thus, Agnes Robins earned the unwelcome distinction of being the first person in Britain killed by a bomb dropped from an aeroplane. She is buried in a family grave at St John's cemetery on Manston Road, Margate.

The inscription on the family grave referring to the death of Agnes Robins is without reference to the fact that she died following an air raid, or that she was the first person killed by a bomb dropped from an aeroplane.

32

Mobile 13-pdr Anti-Aircraft Gun

A surprise for the Zeppelin raiders

The first 13-pdr anti-aircraft gun was an adaptation of the standard horse artillery gun introduced in 1904. The new version, authorised in October 1914, featuring a high-angle mount, was known as the 13-pdr six cwt (13-pdr denoting the weight of the shell fired and six cwt (672lb) the weight of barrel and breech). By mounting some of the guns on lorries they became mobile and proved a useful addition to Britain's anti-aircraft armoury.

As part of a temporary air defence plan in place in October 1915, eight mobile 13-pdr six cwt guns took up selected positions covering the north and eastern approaches to London. The arrangement was to run from 5 to 12 October in anticipation of a possible Zeppelin raid, but when no raid materialised by the final day, the War Office believed the Germans may have discovered the plan. They recalled the guns, but then secret orders followed detailing their redeployment, with two guns positioned in Hertfordshire, four in Essex covering the eastern approaches to London, and two more, one on either side of the Thames, near Woolwich.[35] On

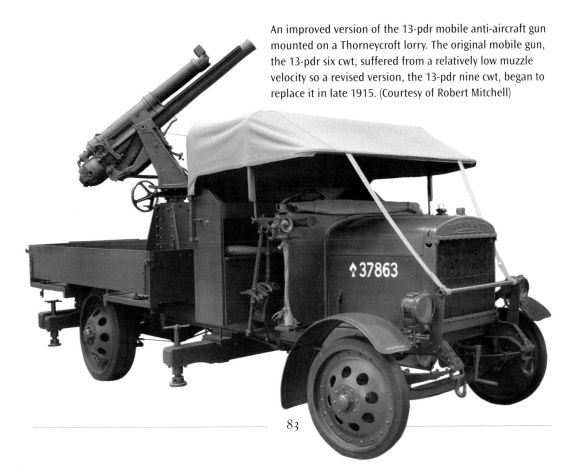

An improved version of the 13-pdr mobile anti-aircraft gun mounted on a Thorneycroft lorry. The original mobile gun, the 13-pdr six cwt, suffered from a relatively low muzzle velocity so a revised version, the 13-pdr nine cwt, began to replace it in late 1915. (Courtesy of Robert Mitchell)

the night of 13 October the Zeppelins returned and all the mobile guns saw action. For the Zeppelin commanders, who whenever possible noted the positions of anti-aircraft guns, this came as a bit of a shock. Joachim Breithaupt, commanding L 15, later recalled: 'We breathed more freely as … we left the City behind us. Then suddenly, as we were about over Leyton [actually Loughton], from a direction in which we had not expected it, a new and murderous fire began.'[36]

The guns, however, were not as effective as had been hoped, due to a relatively low-muzzle velocity. Following calls for an improved gun with a velocity of 2,000 feet per second, in August 1915 a proposal to adapt the 18-pdr gun to fire a 13-pdr shell received approval. To achieve this the barrel of the 18-pdr was reduced in diameter by adding a sleeve inside to accommodate the smaller 13-pdr shell, but by retaining the 18-pdr breech it could still handle the larger charge of the original shell, resulting in increased velocity.

The first delivery of this new version, known as the 13-pdr nine cwt, took place in December 1915; by the end of the war 54 operated within the London Air Defence Area. These guns were generally mounted on either a Daimler or Thorneycroft lorry for the mobile role, an example of which can be seen at the Imperial War Museum, Duxford.

The 13-pdr nine cwt gun. This utilised the breech and barrel of the 18-pdr. By inserting a sleeve inside the barrel the gun could fire the 13-pdr shell using the larger charge from the 18-pdr shell, thus increasing muzzle velocity. (Courtesy of Chris Kolonko)

A very smart unit of the Royal Artillery with a mobile 13-pdr gun. (Courtesy of Chris Kolonko)

33

War Memorial
Hertford, Hertfordshire

Commemorating civilian casualties alongside the military

The Zeppelin raid of 13 October 1915 set out to attack London from all sides but only one raider reached the city. Others attacked towns surrounding London. Zeppelin L 16, commanded by Oberleutnant-zur-See Werner Peterson, lured by lights shining forth from large buildings in Hertford close to the River Lea, mistook them for the East End of London and the Thames and attacked.

His first bombs, seven incendiaries and two high-explosive (HE) bombs, had only a limited impact on property, but the third HE bomb exploded with devastating effect in Bull Plain, a road close to the River Lea.

The names of the victims of the Hertford Zeppelin raid are on a plaque at the base of the town's war memorial alongside those of the military who gave their lives in the war.

The sound of those first two explosive bombs penetrated into the formal surroundings of the Conservative Club at Lombard House on Bull Plain. A number of highly respected local men congregated at the main entrance to investigate the sound just as that third HE bomb exploded in Bull Plain. The blast cut down and killed four of them: James Gregory, an organist and professor of music; John Henry Jevons, borough surveyor; Ernest Thomas Jolly, a bank cashier; and George Cartledge, a draper. A man walking past the club, Charles Spicer, also died. Four other men suffered injuries. A child, George Game, living at No. 37 died in the house and at No. 29 flying window glass injured two women. Many other buildings in Bull Plain suffered broken windows and smashed roof tiles, including the town's museum. Other bombs also claimed lives. In North Road three men died: Arthur Hart, Charles Waller and Arthur Cox.[37]

After the war a public subscription raised money for a memorial for the Hertford men killed in the war. Initially it was not planned to list individual service personal who lost their lives but that decision was overturned and, in addition, the names of the nine victims of the Zeppelin rain were also included. The unveiling on 6 November 1921 must have been a poignant moment for the Mayor of Hertford, Alderman Dr James Burnett-Smith. Not only had he survived a torpedo attack that sank his ship in the Mediterranean while serving as an Army doctor, but also six incendiaries and an HE bomb had fallen in the garden of his house on North Road during the Zeppelin raid. They caused considerable damage but no casualties, although another bomb in the street outside his house was the one that killed Arthur Cox, a bombardier in the Royal Field Artillery.

The Hertford War Memorial, unveiled in November 1921.

Lombard House on Bull Plain. Four men standing here at the entrance to the Conservative Club were killed when a bomb detonated in the street. This historic building is now home to The Hertford Club.

Damage to the home of Dr James Burnett-Smith inflicted during the raid. As mayor of the town, he unveiled the Hertford War memorial in 1921.

34

No. 68 Bus – Aldwych, London

London's West End under attack

The air raid of 13 October 1915 saw Zeppelin L 15, commanded by Kapitänleutnant Joachim Breithaupt, pass over the centre of London.

The first three bombs, all high-explosive (HE), landed in Exeter Street, Wellington Street and Catherine Street, in the theatre district of Covent Garden. An interval in the performance at the Lyceum meant many theatregoers were in the street seeking refreshments when the explosion of the Wellington Street bomb cut down and killed 17 people and injured 21 more.

A No. 68 bus, driven by Charles Tarrant, had just turned off the Strand into Aldwych, heading towards Kingsway, when the first bomb exploded. The conductor, Charles Rogers, was

The registration plate of the No. 68 bus damaged by a fragment of a bomb dropped by Zeppelin L 15 on 13 October 1915. The bus was in Aldwych at the time, heading towards Kingsway. (Courtesy of David Marks)

busy collecting fares from his passengers, among them Edwin Austin and his wife. Mrs Austin recalled: '… there was a loud explosion – and while we were wondering what it was another bomb fell, and another.'[38] Some passengers made a rush to jump off the bus but Mr and Mrs Austin, who were sitting in the front seats on the top deck, stayed where they were. Mr Austin told his wife, 'Stay here, where we are!', and the couple crouched down behind the destination board.

At that moment a fourth HE bomb landed, exploding in Aldwych close to the junction with Drury Lane, and a fifth, just the other side of the Kingsway turning. The bus took the full force of the explosion from the first of these, shrapnel peppering the bodywork and smashing all the windows. Mrs Austin described how they 'felt the concussion of the bombs pass over our heads', but even so both received injuries, that to Mr Austin's leg keeping him in hospital for five weeks. The driver and conductor, however, were not so fortunate. Helpers found Charles Rogers, the conductor, lying dead on the pavement by the bus, his chest ripped open by a jagged bomb fragment that had pierced his lung. The driver, Charles Tarrant, was dying from a large wound in his neck. A troop of Boy Scouts ferrying the injured to hospital picked him up but their leader, Frank Hutton, remembered that Tarrant was 'terribly injured, and died in hospital soon after we got him there'.[39]

A relic of this incident features in the collection of the London Transport Museum – the registration plate of the bus, pierced by shrapnel.

1.Drv.C.J.Tarrant.
2.Drv.F. Kreppell.
3.Cond'r.E.G.Harvey.
4.Cond'r.C. Rogers.

These men met an untimely end, the result of Zeppelin raids.

A postcard showing drivers and conductors killed on London buses in late 1915. Tarrant and Rogers were the crew of the No. 68 stuck by the bomb in Aldwych. (The David Marks Collection)

35

Lincoln's Inn Chapel – London

Visible damage from a Zeppelin bomb

The air raid of 13 October 1915 saw one Zeppelin, L 15 commanded by Kapitänleutnant Joachim Breithaupt, drop its bombs over London from Covent Garden to the East End.

Three of the bombs fell in Lincoln's Inn, one of London's four Inns of Court. The first high-explosive (HE) bomb struck No. 9 New Square, severely damaging the two upper floors of Nos. 8 and 9, and causing further damage throughout the buildings. A second HE bomb fell on the roadway at Old Square just a few feet from the north wall of Lincoln's Inn Chapel, and the third bomb, an incendiary, set fire to the roof of No. 8 Stone Buildings.

The bomb in Old Square caused damage to all the surrounding offices, from Nos. 8 to 14, although not of a particularly serious nature. The impact on the chapel, however, was rather more dramatic. Some fragments from the bomb smashed into the walls of the chapel, while others blasted through archways to the vaulted undercroft. Those that shot upwards smashed through the 17th-century stained glass windows. Outside the chapel those marks remain visible on the wall next to a plaque commemorating the event, with a disc set in the tarmac (both approved in 1922) indicating exactly where the bomb landed. Damage also remains visible in the undercroft.

Two of the windows on the north side of the chapel, towards the western end, were badly smashed and beyond restoration. Although most of the others in the chapel suffered damage,

C. E. Kempe & Co. Ltd. carried out excellent restoration work. From a memorandum written in 1926, we know that some fragments of the

The disc set in the road indicates just how close to the wall of Lincoln's Inn chapel the bomb dropped by Zeppelin L 15 on 8 September 1915 was when it exploded. Unfortunately cars often park over the disc hiding it from view. (Historic Military Press)

broken glass from the two irreparable windows were used in the tracery lights of the repaired windows on the east, north and south sides of the chapel, and impressively, Kempe's were able to recreate the smashed window that had been second from the east on the north side by using broken glass from other windows and reinstated it as the window now third from the east on the north side.[40]

The restored windows, bomb damage to the chapel wall and undercroft, as well as the plaque and road marker, all contribute to making Lincoln's Inn chapel one of London's most visible links with the First Blitz.

The north wall of the chapel peppered by fragments of the bomb dropped by L 15.

The plaque on the wall of Lincoln's Inn Chapel in Old Square explaining the damage to the walls.

An example of the extensive bomb damage visible in the undercroft of the chapel, which opens on to Old Square.

A piece of glass from the
shattered windows of the
chapel in Lincoln's Inn.
(The David Marks Collection)

One small section of the restored window third from the east on the north side of the chapel. The 'crazed'
effect in the glass shows part of the reconstruction. The legs of the left hand figure escaped relatively
unscathed, while those of the figure on the right needed extensive repairs. The fingers of the left hand
figure show signs of repair using a different coloured glass to the rest of the hand.

36

Zeppelin Incendiary Bomb (Naval) Coltishall, Norfolk

One of many bombs dropped on the rural landscape

I n Germany's plan for the raid on the evening of 13 October 1915, five Zeppelins were to attack London from different points of the compass. One, however, Zeppelin L 11, never even came close, even though its commander, Oberleutnant-zur-See Horst von Buttlar, claimed a significant success over east London. His report describes his bombs falling on, 'West Ham, the docks and Woolwich … on dropping the fourth bomb an especially heavy explosion was seen, and three big fires were started which half an hour later still glowed through the light cloud layer.'[41] A dramatic account indeed, but like a number of other reports filed by von Buttlar, it was far from the truth. No bombs fell on east London. The bombs, according to a police report, actually 'plastered Horstead, Coltishall and Great Hautbois', three neighbouring villages between Norwich and the Norfolk coast.

The remains of the 'smouldering beast' incendiary bomb dropped by Zeppelin L 11 and picked up by Harold Neave near Coltishall Station. The fire has burnt away the tarred rope covering. Neave took it home and kept in his shed for many years. It is of the cylindrical design used by Naval Zeppelins. (Courtesy of the Pennoyer Centre)

A report issued by the Chief Constable's Office of the Norfolk Constabulary three days after the raid details L 11's attack:

'About 8.45 a Zeppelin came back over the villages of Horstead, Coltishall and Great Hautbois. This machine dropped 4 explosive and 3 incendiary bombs in Horstead parish, but as they fell in open Fields, they only broke 7 panes of glass. In Coltishall and Great Hautbois they dropped 9 explosive bombs, 2 of which did not explode. All these dropped in open fields not far from the Gt. E. Rly. Station of Coltishall. The only damage done being a tin shed partly blown down and a few panes of glass broken. 7 incendiary bombs were also dropped round 3 cottages, all of which were quickly put out by pails of water.'[42]

One of those wielding the pails of water was Special Constable Harold Neave. Having extinguished one of the burning bombs near Coltishall Station, which he described as a 'smouldering beast', Neave picked it up and, not in keeping with the instructions issued to the police who were to ensure all such items were handed in, took it home as a souvenir. The burnt out bomb remained in Neave's shed for the next 60 years, after which it passed to his family who, in 2011, loaned the bomb to the Pennoyer Centre in Pulham St Mary, Norfolk, where it is currently on display.

Incendiary Bombs

German incendiary bombs contained benzol (petrol) and thermite, a pyrotechnic composition that burns at incredibly high temperatures. Once ignited by an inertia fuse on contact, the thermite rapidly heats

up and burns with an intense heat while spreading burning petrol across the room. Tarred rope wrapped around the bomb keeps it burning after the chemical reaction has died down.

These bombs would smash through the roof and begin fires in the top part of the house, with burning benzol often dripping down through the floorboards. One women in a house struck by an incendiary bomb recalled: 'It was as if a sheet of flame dropped from the ceiling to the floor and shot back again.'

These bombs are sometimes called Goldschmidt bombs after the German chemist, Hans Goldschmidt, who patented the thermite chemical reaction in 1895 and which was used extensively in welding.

A burnt out incendiary bomb of the bell-shaped type used by Army Zeppelins. LZ 38 dropped this one on Ipswich on 30 April 1915.

37

King's Royal Rifle Corps Memorial
Dover, Kent

Evidence of a German air raid

Late in the evening of 22 January 1916, a single Friedrichshafen FF 33b floatplane of *Seeflieger Abteilung 1* left Zeebrugge on the Belgian coast and commenced its 80-mile flight to Dover. The aircraft appeared over the town shortly before 1am, at which point the two-man crew commenced dropping their bombs. The official Press release informed the public: 'Taking advantage of the bright moonlight, a hostile aeroplane visited the East coast of Kent at 1 o'clock this morning, January 23, and, after dropping nine bombs in rapid succession, made off seawards.'[43] With no advance warning of the raid, no searchlights or anti-aircraft guns came into action.

The raider dropped nine bombs. One that struck the Red Lion public house in St James's Street resulted in the death of a man, Harry Sladden, and injuries to three others who were lodging there. Another exploded on the roof of the Phoenix Brewery's malthouse, setting fire to the rafters. One exploded on a wall at the back of Golden Cross Cottages, injuring three children inside No. 10 and a 71-year-old woman, Julia Philpot, at No. 2 Golden Cross Place.[44] But it was the bombs that fell near the King's Royal Rifle Corps Memorial in the south-western portion of the town that have left us with a small but tangible reminder of the raid.

The Rifles Memorial was erected in Dover in 1861 by the First Battalion, King's Royal Rifle Corps, 'in memory of comrades who fell during

The King's Royal Rifle Corps Indian Mutiny Memorial in Dover, with Dover Castle in the background.

the Indian campaigns of 1857, 1858 and 1859' – the Indian Mutiny or Rebellion as known in English or the First War of Independence as favoured in India. The memorial found itself in the front line of this first aerial war when three bombs fell in the surrounding streets: one outside the door of No. 9 Waterloo Crescent, another in the roadway in front of No. 7 Cambridge Terrace and a third that struck the coping of the west wall of No. 1 Camden Crescent. The first two bombs gouged craters about a foot deep and all three combined to smash nearly every window in the area. A fragment of the bomb that had landed in front of Cambridge Terrace flew through the air with great force, striking the edge of the memorial to the right of the bronze trophy and removing a fist-sized chunk of granite, a war wound that remains visible to this day.

ABOVE RIGHT: A close-up of the damage to the memorial, the fist-sized chunk on the left side cut away by a flying fragment of a bomb dropped in Cambridge Terrace in the early hours of 23 January 1916.

BELOW: A postcard showing the area around the memorial as it would have appeared at the time of the raid.

38

Damaged Brickwork
Walsall, West Midlands

Marks of a bomb that killed the Lady Mayoress of Walsall

On the night of 31 January 1916, Germany launched its most ambitious and largest raid so far, with nine Zeppelins aiming to strike against Liverpool. Before this raid, no Zeppelin had penetrated that far inland, so when navigation problems prevented any of the raiders reaching their target, their subsequent attacks over the Midlands were still unexpected and without precedent. Those towns that suffered the Zeppelins' bombs were largely undefended.

Damaged brickwork on a building at the corner of Bradford Street and Newport Street in Walsall. The bomb that inflicted this damage also fatally injured Mary Julia Slater, the Lady Mayoress of Walsall. (Courtesy of Bev Parker)

One of the first Zeppelins to come inland, L 21 commanded by Kapitänleutnant Max Dietrich, had already bombed a number of West Midlands locations, including Tipton, Lower Bradley and Wednesbury, killing 31 people, before approaching Walsall at about 8.25pm. Official records state L 21 dropped seven high-explosive bombs and four incendiaries over the town, killing four people (although two others died from shock brought on by the raid). Three of those died as a result of the final bomb, which exploded in Bradford Place. Two friends, Frank Linney and Charles Cope, were standing in Bradford Place when the bomb cut them down. Linney died later that night and Cope three days later. The bomb also fatally injured the Lady Mayoress of Walsall, Mary Julia Slater, who was on a No. 16 tram with her sister and sister-in-law. The tram had just arrived at Bradford Place when the bomb exploded. Although badly injured, she managed to get out and find her companions, but she had serious injuries to her chest and abdomen and was haemorrhaging badly. Taken to hospital, she remained there for three weeks but never recovered; she died on 20 February of 'shock and septicaemia'. [45]

One piece of the Bradford Place bomb flew in the opposite direction to the tram, striking the wall of the building at the corner of Bradford Street and Newport Street. There the impact gouged out a section of the brickwork. Repairs to that small section of wall were never made and in later years efforts to ensure its preservation have taken place. A wooden frame now surrounds it while alongside is an accompanying plaque explaining its origins.

After the war, the Borough of Walsall erected a memorial to their war dead in the form of a cenotaph, unveiling it in October 1921. The site selected for it was the point where the bomb had exploded in Bradford Place.

After the war the cenotaph in Walsall was erected on the spot where the bomb had exploded in Bradford Place.

39

Granite Bomb Markers
Loughborough, Leicestershire
Remembering bombs that claimed lives

During the big Midlands Zeppelin raid on 31 January 1916, lights showing from the town of Loughborough attracted the attention of one of the last raiders to come inland – L 20, commanded by Kapitänleutnant Franz Stabbert. Just after 8pm, Stabbert released four high-explosive bombs over the town. A bomb that exploded in the middle of The Rushes, a wide road flanked by shops, shocked those in the area. From the ensuing

The granite marker in Empress Road, where a bomb killed five people. Sadly its historical significance escaped the notice of those painting the yellow lines on the road. (Courtesy of Lynne Dyer)

scene of 'unforgettable confusion and horror', amidst the smashed windows, broken shop fronts and tangled telegraph and telephone wires that lay across the street, the bodies of the dead and injured were found. 'A few yards beyond, lay the huddled heap of what a few minutes before had been a woman, and nearby lay her mortally injured husband, conscious and groaning in agony.' The couple were Joseph and Elizabeth Adkin. In a shop doorway, Annie Adcock lay dead and Ethel Higgs, walking home after work, had suffered fatal injuries.[46]

A bomb in Empress Road had a similar tragic impact. The Page family, living at No. 87, heard an explosion from an adjacent street and went out to investigate just as the next bomb exploded outside their neighbour's house. Mary Anne Page and her children, Joseph (aged 18) and Elsie (16), died in the street, their mangled bodies found lying together on the pavement in a pool of blood. The same bomb also killed Arthur Turnill, working at a factory on the other side of the road, and Josiah Gilbert in his shop at No. 77.[47]

After the war, the local council commemorated the loss of lives in The Rushes and Empress Road by setting small squares of local Mountsorrel granite bearing a German cross into the roadway where the two bombs exploded, and placed brass plaques on buildings opposite the markers. Copies bearing the same inscriptions later replaced the original plaques, one of which survives in the Carillon Tower museum. The replacement plaque in The Rushes is no longer in situ but, as part of the centenary commemorations in 2016, a public subscription financed a new bronze plaque for The Rushes created by local artist Paul Gent – the first installed there to list the names of the casualties.

This traffic-worn granite marker can be found embedded in The Rushes, a busy thoroughfare in the town, and marks where a bomb dropped by Zeppelin L 20 exploded, killing four people. (Courtesy of Lynne Dyer)

The original brass plaque erected in The Rushes, opposite the granite marker. It is now in the Carillon Museum, Loughborough. (Courtesy of Charnwood Arts)

The new plaque erected in The Rushes and unveiled on the centenary of the raid on 31 January 2016. (Courtesy of Charnwood Arts)

40

Crown Derby China

A unique mark of a Zeppelin raid

Zeppelin L 14, commanded by Kapitänleutnant der Reserve Alois Böcker, took part in the great Zeppelin raid over the Midlands on the night of 31 January 1916. Böcker got as far west as Shrewsbury in his search for the target, Liverpool, before turning back to the east. Instead of Liverpool, the town of Derby felt the force of L 14's bombs.

Böcker released 21 high-explosive (HE) and four incendiary bombs over the town. Nine of the HE bombs damaged engine sheds at the Midland Railway works, which resulted in the deaths of four men. Other industrial sites suffered, too: the Rolls-Royce works, Litchurch Gas Works, the Metalite Lamp factory and Fletcher's Lace factory. Although the bombs caused damage, no more lives were lost.

Earlier in the evening when word had reached Derby of a possible raid, the town switched off lights, shut down the trams and work came to a halt. At the Old Crown Derby China Works in

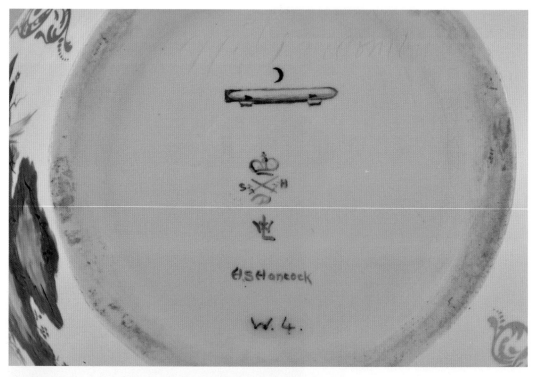

The base of a Crown Derby vase showing the rare Zeppelin mark and crescent moon added to items to commemorate the Zeppelin raid on 31 January 1916. (Courtesy of the Royal Crown Derby Museum)

King Street a kiln loaded with part of a table set of china ordered for the president of Peru had not yet completed its firing when the order came to dowse the fire. Many of those involved feared the short firing would ruin the consignment but when the kiln had cooled in the morning and everything was checked, it was fine. The final batch of items for the set was then placed in the kiln for firing, with any vacant spaces filled with '50 other odds and ends'. The proprietor of the company, William Larcombe, then had an idea to commemorate the Zeppelin raid: 'I instructed our craftsmen to add, in addition to the usual old Crown Derby mark, an impression of a Zeppelin and a crescent moon. This was done and the odds and ends of china were sold together with the usual stock.' Another account implies that the Zeppelin mark was added to those items in the kiln during the raid.[48]

Those 'Zeppelin Mark' pieces of Crown Derby china are now extremely rare and the company's museum only holds two items, and knows of only nine others around the world. They are always keen to hear of the whereabouts of any more.

A Crown Derby vase, decorated with birds and flowers by Harry Sampson Hancock, one of the pieces that bears the rare Zeppelin mark and is now in the Royal Crown Derby Museum. (Courtesy of the Royal Crown Derby Museum)

41

The Trawler King Stephen

Caught up in a net of controversy

Zeppelin L 19, commanded by Kapitänleutnant Odo Loewe, had a troubled night over England during the great raid of 31 January 1916. Although dropping bombs over the West Midlands, she experienced repeated engine failures. On her return journey across the North Sea, she became heavy when Dutch rifle fire from the island of Ameland holed her gas bags. Carried west by strong winds and struggling with further engine problems, L 19 came down in the sea. The helpless crew remained there, clinging to their half-submerged airship until a boat appeared on the morning of 2 February – the Grimsby trawler

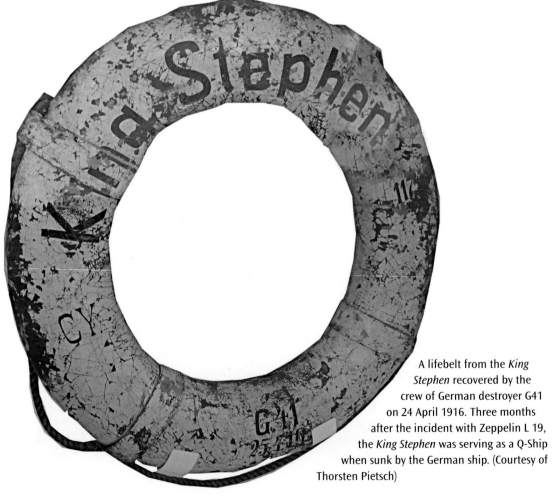

A lifebelt from the *King Stephen* recovered by the crew of German destroyer G41 on 24 April 1916. Three months after the incident with Zeppelin L 19, the *King Stephen* was serving as a Q-Ship when sunk by the German ship. (Courtesy of Thorsten Pietsch)

King Stephen. What followed became one of the most controversial incidents of the First Blitz.

Despite assurances from Loewe that his men would not interfere with the crew of the trawler if they picked them up, the skipper of the *King Stephen*, William Martin, had a difficult decision to make. Estimating the strength of the Zeppelin crew at 30 (in fact there were 16), and with his own nine-man crew unarmed and outnumbered, fearing they would be overpowered and his boat and crew taken to Germany, he decided against taking the risk.

Arriving back at Grimsby the following morning, Martin alerted the authorities, who immediately despatched two destroyers but there was no sign of the downed Zeppelin. A storm had blown up in the night and L 19 had sunk without a trace.

When news of the incident reached Germany, the press there branded Martin a war criminal for leaving the crew to die. At the same time, in Britain, the naval authorities commandeered the *King Stephen*, refitting her as a Q-Ship armed with a 6-pdr Hotchkiss gun and assigned the ship a naval crew under Lieutenant Tom Phillips. But on 24 April 1916, a German destroyer captured and then sank the *King Stephen*, taking her crew into captivity, believing they were the men who abandoned the crew of L 19. Initially the Germans began proceedings to try Phillips as a war criminal but when a newspaper bearing a picture of William Martin was produced the trial collapsed.

Inevitably Germany made much of the propaganda value of the refusal of the *King Stephen* to rescue the crew of L 19, with the production of postcards, paintings, commemorative medallions and damning articles in the press.

The crew of the German destroyer – G 41 – which sank the *King Stephen*, kept a lifebelt as a souvenir. It is now in the collection of the Aeronauticum Museum at Nordholz in Germany.

An artist's impression of the meeting in the North Sea between the crews of the *King Stephen* and Zeppelin L 19.

A German postcard showing the crew of L 19 crammed on the upper machine gun platform angrily shaking their fists at the departing *King Stephen*.

Another German postcard showing the last surviving member of the crew desperately clinging to the sinking remains of Zeppelin L 19. (The David Marks Collection)

42

The Manchester Regiment Memorial
Cleethorpes, Lincolnshire
A tragic air raid incident

Zeppelin L 22, one of seven raiders that set out to attack England on 31 March 1916, experienced severe engine problems during the crossing of the North Sea and, abandoning plans to attack London, set course for the Humber.

Having dropped bombs over Humberston, the commander of L 22, Kapitänleutnant Martin Dietrich, steered towards Cleethorpes, which he believed was Grimsby. Once over the town he dropped three high-explosive bombs, while three others landed harmlessly in fields. Of those in the town, one landed on the pavement in Sea View Road, smashing windows in houses and shops. One struck a wing of the Town Hall, damaging council offices in Cambridge Street, and one in Alexandra Road destroyed a Baptist chapel. By a stroke of misfortune, during the day 84 soldiers of the 3rd Battalion (Special Reserve) The Manchester Regiment had arrived in the town to bolster the coastal defences. The chapel hall housed 70 men of 'E' company and 14 men of 'A' company took up billets in neighbouring shops. At 1.48am on 1 April, when most of the men had bedded down for the night, the bomb detonated on impact with the slate roof of the chapel. It demolished approximately half of the roof, a large part falling into the building where the men were billeted. The explosion also blasted the upper part of the wall and the copingstone off the north end, which

The Manchester Regiment memorial in Cleethorpes cemetery. (Courtesy of Paul Reed)

smashed through the corrugated iron roof of the shops to crush the men of 'A' Company quartered there.[49] When rescuers had finished picking their way through the horrific scene of destruction and carnage, only four of the 84 men were discovered to be untouched by the blast – they had sneaked away to a cellar for a game of cards. Rescuers removed the bodies of 27 dead soldiers from the wreckage, one more died later that day and three more of their injuries within a few days. One man, Private Thomas Stott, eventually succumbed two months later, on 2 June 1916, leaving the final casualty total at 32 killed and 48 injured.

At the funeral on 4 April 1916, 24 of the bodies were laid to rest in two graves at Cleethorpes cemetery. Another soldier, Private William Bodsworth, who died that day, was later buried with them. The other seven bodies, including that of Private Stott, were returned to their home towns for burial. A memoriam card issued in time for the funeral shows 29 names, all those that had died by 3 April.

Two years later, on 9 March 1918, a memorial erected by public subscription was unveiled to the victims of the raid, listing on three stone panels the names of 31 of the 32 killed. Sadly, as was the case with other memorial lists, Private Stott became the forgotten victim.

Close-up of the names of those killed in the raid. (Courtesy of Paul Reed)

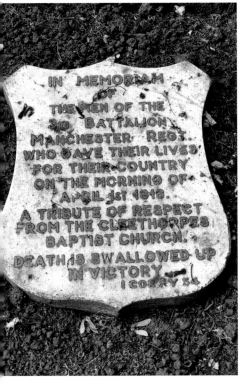

ABOVE: The original entrance to the Baptist Chapel at Cleethorpes, built in 1910, survived the destructive blast of the bomb dropped by Zeppelin L 22. (Courtesy of Paul Reed)

LEFT: The stone shield laid in front of the memorial by the Baptist Chapel as a 'tribute of respect'. (Courtesy of Paul Reed)

Men of the 3rd Batt. Manchester Regt.
Who gave their lives for their Country

No. 33055	Lc-Cpl.	Swift, J.
„ 32323	„	Haynes, C.
„ 30358	Pte.	Ball, W.
„ 34637	„	Beaumont, L. A.
„ 32238	„	Beardsley, Joseph
„ 9779	„	Bell, S.
„ 30117	„	Brierley, T.
„ 34621	„	Brown, W. H.
„ 34619	„	Budding, E.
„ 32194	„	Chandler, F.
„ 32997	„	Chandler, J.
„ 34618	„	Clowes, J.
„ 34633	„	Cuthbert, H.
„ 30241	„	Dimelow, F.
No. 30401	„	Diveney, T.
„ 32215	„	Downs, A. E.
„ 34620	„	Fox, R.
„ 32034	„	Francis, W.
„ 32263	„	Hannon, T.
„ 33107	„	Harrison, P.
„ 30126	„	Hetherington, W.
„ 32278	„	Pierce, T.
„ 27724	„	Radford, J.
„ 27902	„	Ramsden, H.
„ 30179	„	Russell, J.
„ 32275	„	Tomkinson, T.
„ 27591	„	Wheeler, J.
„ 34639	„	Wild, W.
„ 27537	„	Wood R.

Laid to rest in Cleethorpes Cemetery, April 4th, 1916.

The 'In memoriam' card giving the names of the victims of the Cleethorpes Baptist Chapel bomb who had died by 3 April; three more died later. (The David Marks Collection)

43

The Wakefield Medal

A shared reward for bringing down a Zeppelin

Such was the dominance of the Zeppelins in the autumn of 1915, that after his election as Lord Mayor of London in November, Sir Charles Wakefield offered a prize of £500 (worth close to £50,000 today) to any person or persons instrumental in bringing down a Zeppelin over the British Isles. As a wealthy businessman he did this in a private capacity.

On the night of 31 March 1916, Zeppelin L 15 had come inland over Suffolk intending to strike against London. Heading south, her commander, Kapitänleutnant Joachim Breithaupt, sighted the Thames when he reached Pitsea in Essex and turned to follow it towards London. A searchlight at Perry Street near Gravesend was first to locate L 15, and within the next few minutes more lights opened and 11 guns began bombarding the sky all around her. Breithaupt tried to get away, releasing 44 bombs over fields at Rainham to lighten his ship and help it climb rapidly, but it was too late. A shell credited to the 3-inch 20 cwt gun at Purfleet burst close by, slashing open three or four of L 15's central gas cells. Breithaupt hoped to nurse his ailing ship home, but the loss of hydrogen meant she began to lose height. Despite jettisoning all excess weight, L 15's back broke and she fell from a height of 2,000 feet into the sea about 15 miles north of Margate. One man drowned but ships quickly reached the scene and picked up the rest of the crew.

The Wakefield medal awarded to Gunner R. Evans. Originally issued as a plain medal, many recipients added a fixing so the medal could be worn. (Courtesy of the Southend Museum)

The forlorn hulk of Zeppelin L 15 at sea about 15 miles north of Margate after damage inflicted by AA gun fire forced her down.

The officer commanding the Purfleet guns, Captain Joseph Harris, Royal Garrison Artillery, wrote to claim the £500 prize for his men. Wakefield forwarded his letter to the War Office for verification but it baulked at the idea of

servicemen receiving financial prizes and, after an investigation, they deemed that other guns had claims, too. As a solution, Wakefield engaged Mappin & Webb to produce a number of 9-carat gold medallions for distribution to the gun and searchlight crews involved in the action. Ready by November 1916, 353 of the medallions were issued.[50] Each bore the name of the recipient on the reverse, with an image of an AA gun and the name L 15, while a scroll bore the words, 'Well Hit – March 31st – April 1st 1916'. The obverse carried the words, 'Presented by the Lord Mayor of London – Colonel Sir Charles Wakefield', and his coat of arms. It appears that no official list of recipients has survived.

Charles Wakefield earned his fortune from producing lubricating oils for automobile and aeroplane engines. By adding castor oil to his product he developed an oil that was runny enough to work from cold at start-up and thick enough to keep working at very high temperatures. He called his new oil, Castrol. In later years Sir Charles became a great philanthropist and this relief bust is on the wall of a house he lived in at 41 Trinity Square, London, but which in 1937 he donated to 'charitable causes'.

44

Ranken Dart

A weapon in the anti-Zeppelin arsenal

On the night of 31 March 1916, the AA guns along the Thames received credit for bringing down Zeppelin L 15. However, another weapon in the anti-Zeppelin arsenal also came into play – Ranken darts.

In June 1915, a Royal Navy Engineer lieutenant-commander, Frances Ranken, began working on an idea for an anti-Zeppelin weapon, and the following month the Royal Naval Air Service accepted his explosive missile, the Ranken dart. After further tests in February 1916, the Royal Flying Corps also approved their use.[51]

The darts were about 12 inches long, one inch wide and weighed just under 1lb. They contained an explosive charge in the forward section and black powder in the rear. Ignition was by means of a friction tube. At the rear of the dart three spring-loaded vanes opened when released from the aircraft. The principle of the design was that the iron tip penetrated the outer fabric of the Zeppelin, on which the vanes caught hold. A wire coil provided a delay action, allowing the leading section to penetrate about 18 inches inside the Zeppelin before the friction tube ignited the explosive.

Held in tin boxes containing 24 darts, the pilot could release them in batches of three, or all 24 together. For the pilot who encountered L 15, 2nd Lieutenant Alfred de Bathe Brandon, the experience was a series of fast-moving, confusing encounters in the dark. 'I circled round in front, and climbed, and passed over the Zeppelin I think at about three to four hundred feet, and dropped No. 1 lot of darts. I heard three reports and thought I had made a hit.'[52]

Ranken dart with vanes deployed. The idea being that the body of the dart would penetrate the Zeppelin's outer envelope and the vanes hold it in place prior to it exploding.

The Zeppelin, however, was still intact. Ahead of L 15 now, Brandon turned back and, taking his eye off the target for a moment, readied an incendiary bomb. When he looked up he recalled: 'I was astonished to find that in a very few seconds I would have passed the Zeppelin, so I quickly placed the incendiary bomb in my lap, and let off No. 2 and 3 lots of darts'.

Disappointedly Brandon heard no explosions. He turned his aircraft around again to make a third attack, but Zeppelin L 15 had now disappeared into the night. Despite the failure of the Ranken darts to bring down L 15, the damage from the AA guns proved critical and she would not get back to Germany.

A Ranken dart with vanes stowed prior to their release, and a cutaway section.

2nd Lieutenant Alfred de Bathe Brandon of No. 19 Reserve Aeroplane Squadron who unsuccessfully deployed Ranken darts against Zeppelin L 15 on 31 March 1916. Two weeks later the squadron became No. 39 (Home Defence) Squadron. (The David Marks Collection)

45

Zeppelin L 15 Relics

Mementoes of the first Zeppelin brought down within reach of Britain

After its encounter with the anti-aircraft guns along the Thames and the attack by 2nd Lieutenant Brandon with Ranken darts, Zeppelin L 15 came down in the sea about 15 miles north of Margate, not far from the Kentish Knock lightship. With its back broken, 17 men of the crew made their way onto the nose of L 15 and there awaited their fate – one man was missing. About an hour later the armed trawler *Olivine* transferred the men to the destroyer HMS *Vulture*, which conveyed them to Chatham as POWs.

Before plans for a salvage operation were in place, Mr Tibbenham, one of the crew of the lightship, took some of the duralumin wreckage; he made it into brooches for the ladies in his family.[53] Souvenirs of this type became extremely popular as the war progressed.

A salvage crew led by Chief Gunner (T) W. A. Austin, aboard the armed trawler *Seamew*, located and buoyed the wreck on 6 April, pulling up a 30-foot tail section from a depth of 90 feet. Three days later, having put nets around the wreck, *Seamew* and three other trawlers began to tow the wreckage towards the shore, but after about a mile the towing wires broke. Various attempts over the next few weeks, often hampered by bad weather, suffered a similar fate and it was not until 28 May that the wreckage was hauled onto Margate Sand, a sandbank lying off Margate and Westgate.[54]

Each day at low tide salvage teams sifted through the wreckage and, up to 8 June, Austin reported that, 'numerous parts had been sent in, including 5 canvas bags, one metal case of charts, 2 propellers with shaft and gear boxes, one machine gun, bomb dropping machines, instruments and

Crosses made from Zeppelin wreckage were popular souvenirs. This one belonged to Lieutenant Commander William Johnston, Royal Navy, who went out to see the wreck before the salvage operation commenced. (Courtesy of Ian Campbell)

control and steering gear'. They also recovered the body of Willy Albrecht, the missing crewman. Soon after, however, Austin reported that, 'owing to the shifting nature of the Margate Sand the remains of the wreckage have now disappeared'.

During the salvage operation many pieces of the wreckage ended up in the hands of local people and a lively trade in souvenirs developed, much of the metal worked up into badges, brooches, and other decorative items. This trend continued at subsequent Zeppelin crash sites, the British public developing an insatiable desire to possess a piece of one of the ill-fated Zeppelin raiders.

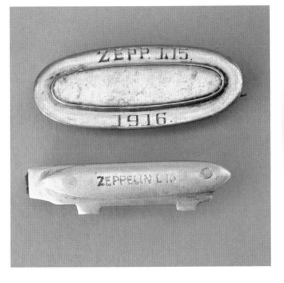

ABOVE LEFT: Two small brooches made from pieces of the duralumin wreckage of L 15.

ABOVE RIGHT: An unusual L 15 souvenir, made in the shape of an anvil and mounted on a wooden plinth. (The David Marks Collection)

RIGHT: A postcard produced 'In never loving memory' of Zeppelin L 15 to commemorate its destruction by British guns. (The David Marks Collection)

In Never
Lioving Memory
OF L-15.

Laid to Rest in the Thames Estuary, April Fool's Day, 1916.

Here lie the remains of a raiding Zep,
Which from Germany came while our children slept,
Our Terriers gallantly manned their guns,
And brought down the cultured murdering Huns,
To whom we can say should we near them be,
"Go to *L-15*—at the bottom of the sea."

46

Carbonit High-Explosive Bomb
Edinburgh, Scotland

The standard Zeppelin bomb used by Naval Zeppelins

The standard high-explosive (HE) bomb dropped by German Navy Zeppelins was the Carbonit type, which continued in use throughout the war. Developed by the firm Sprengstoff A. G. Carbonit, with headquarters at Hamburg and manufacturing plants at Kiel and at Schlebusch, they produced their distinctive teardrop-shaped bombs in various sizes. The most common size employed by Navy Zeppelins was the 50kg, sometimes supported by the 100kg version and occasionally with the 300kg bomb. The designers believed that the shape of the cast-iron body, with its low centre of gravity, would help accuracy but there are reports that the bomb oscillated in flight despite the ring-shaped stabiliser at the tail. Positioned within the stabilising ring was a propeller-activated fuse and a handle attached to the ring allowed the bomb to be held in an electronically activated bomb release (introduced in new Zeppelins from April 1915) controlled from the command gondola. The nose of the bomb was made of steel to aid penetration.

On the night of 2 April 1916, Zeppelins raided Scotland for the first time, with Zeppelin L 14 dropping bombs on Leith and the city of Edinburgh. Of the 43 bombs recorded, 26 were Carbonit HE bombs, of which two failed to detonate. The National Museum of Flight at East Fortune airfield has an unexploded bomb

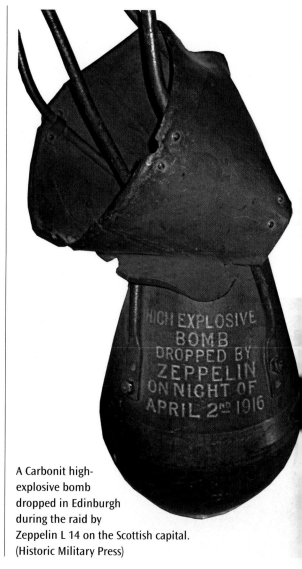

A Carbonit high-explosive bomb dropped in Edinburgh during the raid by Zeppelin L 14 on the Scottish capital. (Historic Military Press)

from the raid in its collection. One unexploded bomb landed on a railway siding in Leith and the other struck a tenement at No. 82 Marchmont Crescent in Edinburgh, smashing through the roof and crashing down through three floors of the building. It is not possible to be certain which bomb is on display. The museum believes their bomb to be the one that struck Marchmont Crescent, however, it appears intact and the police report states that 'a large portion of the shell' penetrated down through the building, suggesting that the bomb broke up.[55]

Other bombs falling on Edinburgh that night are also remembered. A flagstone in Grassmarket outside the White Lion Hotel indicates where a Carbonit HE bomb exploded. It caused extensive damage and injured four people, one of whom later died. Another bomb just missed Edinburgh Castle, landing instead on the south-west slopes of Castle Rock. The explosion sent out a shower of rock and bomb fragments that smashed windows in Castle Terrace, Grindlay Street and Spittal Street. A plaque on the slopes marks the point where the bomb struck.

RIGHT: An inscribed flagstone in Grassmarket marks where a bomb exploded outside the White Lion Hotel. (Courtesy of Mark Lawley)

BELOW LEFT: A great crowd of sightseers in Grassmarket gather around the White Lion Hotel to see the bomb damage.

BELOW RIGHT: The plaque high on Castle Rock, which marks the spot where a bomb exploded, just missing Edinburgh Castle. (Courtesy of Kevin Kelly)

47

The Bomb on Lauriston Place
Edinburgh, Scotland
A family's narrow escape

Of the 26 high-explosive bombs (HE) that fell on Leith and Edinburgh on the night of 2/3 April 1916, one struck a house at No. 39 Lauriston Place. According to police reports, this was the third bomb to hit Edinburgh, the first exploding in Bellevue Terrace (HE) and the second falling in the roadway of The Mound (incendiary). The four-storey house in Lauriston Place was home to Dr John McLaren and his family: his wife, their three children, John, Evelyn, Alastair, and two maids. The house next door, at No. 41, was utilised from 1913 as a school for children infected by the skin disease ringworm – known locally as the 'Skins School'.

Dr McLaren's son, nine-year-old Alastair, kept a diary and wrote of the night the bomb fell on the house. Aware of the thud of exploding bombs gradually getting closer, Dr McLaren and his wife then heard the sound of one that appeared to be overhead and falling towards them. The doctor said starkly to his wife, 'this has got us'. In his diary Alastair wrote:

'He was right. The bomb exploded on the roof almost mid-way between 39, us, and 41, the Skins School. It blew off most of the roof, blew out all the plate-glass windows, and the nose of the bomb, a large lump of steel, continued through all the floors of the house until it reached the pantry where the stone floor stopped it. Needless to say I was awakened by this explosion and was very frightened but did not cry.'[56]

Amazingly, no one was injured. Outside in the street, however, the outcome was different. A fragment of the bomb streaked through the air for about 80 yards before slashing into the abdomen of David Robertson, a 27-year-old discharged soldier. He died of his injuries.

The nose cone of the bomb that penetrated through No. 39 Lauriston Place and came to rest against the stone floor of the pantry. (Courtesy of Dr Hamish McLaren)

Back at No. 39 Lauriston Place, once morning light had illuminated the chaos of damage to their home, Evelyn, Dr McLaren's daughter, is reputed to have remarked, with some understatement, that it would be sometime before they got breakfast. Very aware of their fortunate escape, Mrs McLaren kept part of a sideboard damaged by the bomb and had the nose cone, recovered from the pantry, mounted. She added a silver plaque bearing the words, 'LEST WE FORGET'. The family never has.

ABOVE LEFT: Part of the sideboard kept by the family through which a portion of the bomb passed. (Courtesy of Dr Hamish McLaren)

ABOVE RIGHT: Damage in one of the bedrooms at No. 39 Lauriston Place. (Courtesy of Dr Hamish McLaren)

The explosion of the bomb caused a thick layer of dust to settle over everything in the house. These finger drawings were made on a bedroom door by Dr John McLaren's eldest son, also John but known in the family as Ian. They show the Kaiser and a Zeppelin dropping bombs. (Courtesy of Dr Hamish McLaren)

48

Bombs on Danby High Moor
North Yorkshire Moors
A major bombardment of a windswept moor

Throughout the war only one place in Britain can claim the distinction of coming under attack by four Zeppelins on the same night. It is easy to imagine this would be London or a major industrial centre but not so. On a night when navigation proved extremely difficult, the recipient of this concentrated attack was the wide open spaces of the windswept North Yorkshire Moors.

During the raid on the night of 2/3 May 1916, five Zeppelins appeared over Yorkshire. The first, Zeppelin L 23, came inland over Robin Hood's Bay and headed west. Her commander, Kapitänleutnant Otto von Schubert, dropped a single incendiary bomb as he passed over Danby High Moor at 9.40pm. Commanders often dropped single incendiary bombs that, when ignited, could be an aid to calculating ground speed and drift. Landing among the heather on this remote moorland, the fire created by the bomb began to spread. Thinking no more of it, Von Schubert then turned north and prepared to attack the Skinningrove Iron Works.

A little under an hour later, Oberleutnant-zur-See Werner Peterson, commanding Zeppelin L 16, was passing over the moors when he saw a large fire to the north, which he calculated was at Stockton-on-Tees. As he approached, Peterson looked on as another Zeppelin started bombing 'Stockton' and he confidently observed, 'well-placed hits on buildings at the site of the fire'. This other Zeppelin, L 17, having already dropped bombs near the coast, was attacking what her commander, Kapitänleutnant Herbert Ehrlich, described as a 'coastal city'. But both commanders were wrong – their bombs rained down on the heather fire now burning wildly on Danby High Moor.

At about the same time, Zeppelin L 13, commanded by Kapitänleutnant Eduard Prölss, crossed the coast at Whitby and headed inland. Although trackers found it difficult to follow the Zeppelin's movements, she passed over the moors and with the huge blaze the only source of light in a blackened landscape, it appears likely that Prölss also bombed the fire as only two other bombs were traced to L 13 that night.[57]

Official estimates state that seven incendiaries fed the huge heather fire and that there were 'at least 39 HE bombs' of which 'the majority landed on boggy ground, and none did any damage whatever'.[58] A local report, however, states there was damage inflicted to some cattle sheds. It was not the result Germany had hoped for.

ABOVE: Two fragments from one of the 'at least' 39 high-explosive bombs dropped on Danby High Moor on the night of 2/3 May 1916. The label states they were recovered from Danby Dale Head. (Courtesy of David Marks)

OVERLEAF: Contemporary map of the Danby Moor area. The area around Danby Dale Head, from where the bomb fragments were recovered, is circled. The North Yorkshire Moors archaeological officer has also identified some faint crater-like features and a number of small ponds (approx. four to five metres across) in this area; these could be the result of bombs, although this is not proven.

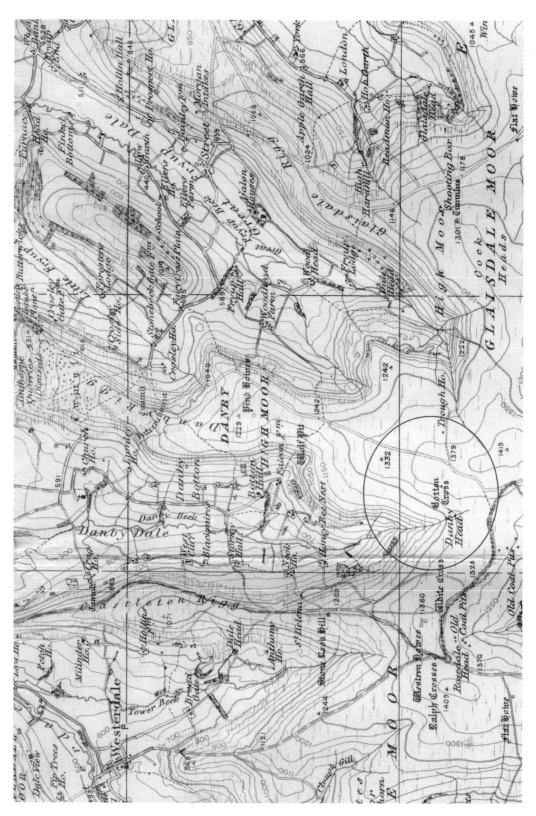

49

A Souvenir of Zeppelin L 20

A long-distance Zeppelin excursion to the shores of Loch Ness

Loch Ness in the Highlands of Scotland is more commonly associated with denizens of the deep rather than aerial monsters, but on the night of 2 May 1916 a Zeppelin appeared over the dark waters of the fabled beast's lair.

The commander of Zeppelin L 20, Kapitänleutnant Franz Stabbert, came inland between Montrose and Arbroath, hoping to reach the Firth of Forth by taking advantage of a tail wind. Sometime later he became aware that the wind had veered. Flying over a solid cloud base he could not discover where he was or where the wind was pushing him; a perilous situation made worse by heavy rain and snow squalls. Only at about midnight, when the clouds finally cleared, was he able to discern where he was – Loch Ness! He immediately turned about and set course back to the coast. At about 1.45am, after flying over an endless black landscape, Stabbert saw lights. Believing it to be a mine pithead, he dropped six high-explosive bombs. The bombs did not find an industrial target, instead they landed in the grounds of Craig Castle at Rhynie. With no fear of a Zeppelin attack this far north, the owners had their generator-powered electric lights illuminated. Fortunately all the bombs missed the castle, although at least one exploded within 40 feet of the building. No one was hurt but the bombs smashed windows and damaged the roof.[59] It was one of the more unusual targets of the First Blitz.

The crew of L 20 had a miserable end to their night. Unable to get back to Germany because of a shortage of fuel after their long detour, Stabbert took the decision to head for neutral Norway, where they crash-landed in a fjord. Fate then took a hand. Ten of the crew made their own way ashore

A napkin ring made from the wreckage of Zeppelin L 20. It bears the inscription, 'Zepp. L.20 Hafrsfjord Mai 1916'. (Courtesy of the Tangmere Military Aviation Museum)

but six were rescued from the icy water by civilian fishing boats; the Norwegians deemed those six to be 'shipwrecked mariners' and repatriated them to Germany, while the other ten were interned. Souvenirs from the wreckage of L 20 are rare – the piece shown here, fashioned into a napkin ring, is in the collection of the Tangmere Military Aviation Museum, West Sussex.

Back in 1971 a feature film was released called *Zeppelin*. It is a fictional tale of a Zeppelin flying to the Highlands and landing a raiding party to attack a remote Scottish castle where the Government has stored priceless historic documents including the Magna Carta. Zeppelins over the Highlands seemed a bit far-fetched to me at the time, but one is left to wonder if the team behind the film were aware of the story of L 20, using it as the basis for a more fantastic cinematic tale of derring-do much in vogue at the time.

Craig Castle at Rhynie, Aberdeenshire, the surprising target for six bombs dropped by Zeppelin L 20 in the early hours of 3 May 1916. (Courtesy of Richard Paxman)

A beautifully colourised image of the wreck of Zeppelin L 20, in Hafrsfjord, Norway, on 3 May 1916. Unable to get back to Germany after its long flight over Scotland, L 20 ditched in the fjord. (Original image by Hans Henriksen /Stavanger City Archive. © Colourised by Tom Marshall (PhotograFix) 2018)

50

Explosive and Incendiary Bullets

The weapon that ended the Zeppelin menace

During the first full year of Zeppelin attacks, the main anti-Zeppelin weapons were bombs and Ranken darts, both needing a height advantage for deployment. Zeppelins, however, could easily outclimb the available British aircraft.

A false belief that a layer of inert gas between the outer envelope and the hydrogen gas cells protected them from incendiary attack initially hindered official attempts to find a method for igniting the hydrogen. The problem was that although hydrogen is highly flammable, it only becomes so when mixed with oxygen, so while the hydrogen is contained within its gas cell it is inert. Three men, working independently, finally found a way to strike at the Zeppelin's Achilles' heel.[60]

At the start of the war, a Coventry-based engineer and experienced chemist, James Buckingham, turned his attention to developing a phosphorus incendiary bullet. He gave a successful demonstration of a .45 incendiary bullet in April 1915 and later developed a .303 version for machine guns, delivering a trial batch to the Admiralty on 12 October 1915; two weeks later they placed a first order for the Royal Naval Air Service. On 27 April 1916 an order followed for the Royal Flying Corps.

John Pomeroy, an inventor from New Zealand, created his first explosive bullet in 1902 but for many years was unable to generate any interest in it. He offered it to Britain on three occasions without success, the last of these in September 1915. Three months later, however, the Munitions Invention Department agreed to trials, which led to the Royal Flying Corps placing an initial order in May 1916.

Meanwhile, Flight Lieutenant Frank Brock of the Intelligence Section of the Admiralty's Air Department, had also begun work on an explosive bullet that also offered an incendiary element. At an initial trial in October 1915 it showed promise and after further trials the Admiralty placed its first order for the Brock bullet in February 1916. The Royal Flying Corps followed suit in April, but later returned

The bullets that changed the air war over Britain. From left to right: Brock (complete and in section), Pomeroy (complete and in section) and Buckingham (complete and in section). (Courtesy of Ian Jones MBE)

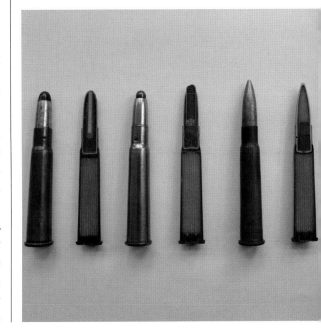

James Buckingham (on the right), the inventor and manufacturer of the Buckingham incendiary bullet. Before the war Buckingham designed and built successful cycle-cars; the photo shows him in one of his vehicles, the Buckingham Chota. (Courtesy of Antony Anderson)

A member of the famous Brock Fireworks family, Flight Lieutenant Frank Brock, RNAS, used his knowledge of explosives to devise the Brock bullet, one of the three successfully employed against German airships in the latter part of 1916.

the majority of their Brock bullets as they felt they were too sensitive and favoured the Pomeroy type.

No one bullet on its own could guarantee success but when all three were loaded together in the 97-round Lewis machine gun magazine they proved lethal, with the explosive bullets able to open large holes in the gas bags and the incendiary bullets igniting the now volatile hydrogen. In the autumn of 1916 these bullets marked the beginning of the end of the Zeppelin menace.

A rare photograph of John Pomeroy, the dogged inventor of the Pomeroy bullet. Reproduced in an Australian newspaper in 1931, 15 years after his bullet was adopted by the RFC, this photo seems to be the earliest public image of him.

RIGHT: Developed by Major Lanoe Hawker, VC, and Air Mechanic W. L. French, the 'double-drum' 97-round magazine for use with the aircraft mounted Lewis machine gun entered service in 1916. The strap allowed the changing of the drum while wearing thick gloves. (Courtesy of Arundel Militaria)

LEFT: The underside of the 97-round drum with the first two bullets in place and the third being loaded. The loading process was carried out by hand. (Courtesy of Arundel Militaria)

51

'Super Zeppelin' Gondolas

The new Zeppelin class – bigger than anything that had gone before

Throughout the war new classes of Zeppelin became available, developed in response to British defensive improvements. In March 1915, before the first 'p-class' appeared, the Navy requested a new bigger airship but with the proviso that it would still fit in the largest available airship sheds. The Naval authorities, unimpressed with the designs, issued another order in July 1915 calling for a six-engined airship without limitation by shed size, with complementary instructions being issued for the enlargement of sheds already under construction and for the building of new ones measuring 790 feet in length. The first airship of this design – the r-class – began construction in February 1916 at the Friedrichshafen Zeppelin works and reached completion at the end of May.[61] First off the production line, L 30 was a giant step forward.

Measuring 649 feet seven inches in length, this new Zeppelin was 113 feet longer than

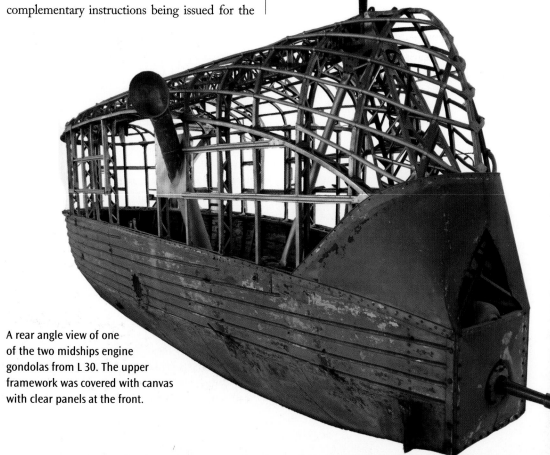

A rear angle view of one of the two midships engine gondolas from L 30. The upper framework was covered with canvas with clear panels at the front.

the 'p-class' and 64 feet longer than the interim 'q-class'. Its diameter measured 78 feet five inches, an increase of 17 feet over both the two preceding classes. This increased body size raised the hydrogen capacity from 1,126,400 cubic feet to an immense 1,949,600 cubic feet. The increased hydrogen gave the L 30 a useful lift of about 27 tons, a significant increase over the 'p-class' at 15 tons. Useful lift covered the weight of crew, supplies, fuel, oil, water ballast, machine guns and bombs. With this load the 'r-class' could still attain a height of 13,000 feet over Britain (about two and a half miles). The six Maybach engines delivered a maximum speed of 62mph in trials, with one accommodated in the rear section of the control gondola, one each in the two side gondolas and three housed in the rear gondola.[62] The British dubbed these the 'Super Zeppelins'.

L 30 raided England on 9 August and 2 September without significant effect and although her commander claimed other raids, British records do not substantiate this. May 1917 saw L 30 transferred to Seerappen in East Prussia, serving there until decommissioning in November 1917. She remained in the shed until war reparations saw her handed over to Belgium in 1920. Belgium, having no airship sheds or crew available, broke her up but brought back some parts, which are now on display in the Aviation Hall of Brussels' Royal Museum of the Armed Forces and Military History.

A front angle view of the midships engine gondola. The gondola housed one Maybach HSLu 240hp engine.

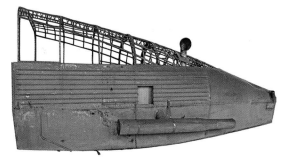

A side view of the rear portion of the rear engine gondola of L 30. Inside were three Maybach HSLu 240hp engines driving three propellers. In total the 'r-class' had six engines: one positioned at the rear of the command gondola, two in midships gondolas and three in the rear gondola.

The first of the 'r-class' type, Zeppelin L 30, known to the British as the 'Super Zeppelins'. L 30 entered service with the Naval Airship Division on 30 May 1916 and made its first raid on England later that year on the night of 8/9 August.

52

Royal Aircraft Factory B.E.2c
Outclassed on the Western Front but an ideal Zeppelin fighter

The most effective aircraft in the war against the Zeppelins proved to be the B.E.2c (Blériot Experimental). Originally designed by the Royal Aircraft Factory as an extremely stable platform ideally suited to front-line reconnaissance and aerial photography, its lack of manoeuvrability made it vulnerable when Germany introduced the Fokker *Eindecker* fighter in the second half of 1915. The German pilots began to refer to the B.E.2c as *kaltes Fleisch* (cold meat). Back in England, however, the stability of the B.E.2c proved a beneficial quality when sent up into the night sky to seek Zeppelins.

B.E.2c No. 2699 was for many years on display at the Imperial War Museum in London but now resides at IWM Duxford. No. 2699 served with No. 50 (Home Defence) Squadron, RFC, which formed in May 1916, and its first confirmed patrol took place on the night of 2/3 August 1916, when the squadron's commanding officer, Major Malcolm Christie, took off at

An immaculate B.E.2c – No. 2699 – that saw Home Defence service in 1916 and 1917 with No. 50 Squadron.

1.45am from Dover. By the time he was airborne the only Zeppelin to appear over Kent that night had already turned for home.[63]

Christie piloted 2699 again from Dover on the night of 24/25 August 1916 and, although he caught a glimpse of Zeppelin L 32, he lost sight of her in cloud.[64] During the Zeppelin raid of 23/24 September 1916, 2699 was flown by Lieutenant W. Glenny.[65] Transferred to the squadron's airfield at Throwley, her next confirmed flight took place on 16 March 1917, with 2nd Lieutenant Anthony Arkell at the controls. Arkell flew through three rainstorms before engine problems forced him to land.[66] Arkell flew from Throwley again on the night of 23 May 1917 to oppose a Zeppelin raid, but heavy rain curtailed his flight.[67] With new improved aircraft joining the squadron, it proved to be 2699's last combat mission. She transferred to No. 190 (Night) Training Squadron in April 1918 and then to No. 192 (Night) Training Squadron in October of that year. After the war, the RAF transferred 2699 to No. 51 Squadron but, following a flight on 13 May 1919 during which 2699 needed to make a forced landing, she was withdrawn from service and shortly afterwards handed over to the fledgling Imperial War Museum.[68]

Although B.E.2c No. 2699 never encountered a Zeppelin, others did, shooting down five German airships between 3 September and 28 November 1916.

Malcolm Christie, commander of No. 50 (Home Defence) Squadron, flew BE2c No.2699 on a least two occasions while searching for Zeppelins.

53

Severndroog Castle
Shooter's Hill, London

An 18th century folly with a 20th century anti-Zeppelin role

Severndroog Castle, standing on the highest point in south London, is not a castle at all, rather it is an 18th-century folly built by the widow of Sir William James in 1784 as a memorial to her husband. He had earned fame in 1755 when leading the naval forces of the East India Company in a successful attack on the island fortress of Suvarnadurg (rendered in English as Severndroog). In 1914 the land on Shooter's Hill on which the tower stands formed part of the estate of Castle Wood House, from where it played an important role in the defence of London.

When the war broke out in 1914, Britain's police forces recruited great numbers of volunteer Special Constables to support the regular police and who were given the task of guarding vulnerable points in their own districts. These included places such as waterworks, power

Severndroog Castle at Shooter's Hill, London. From its lofty position overlooking London, Severndroog Castle proved an ideal observation post from where Special Constables could report on the progress of enemy aircraft.

stations, bridges and telephone exchanges. Later they manned observation posts, reporting on approaching enemy aircraft. Due to its location, just two miles from Woolwich Arsenal, and with unhindered views across London and its approaches, Severndroog Castle became one of the most important observation posts south of the Thames.

Located within the boundaries of 'R' Division of the Metropolitan Police, the responsibility for manning the tower at night fell to Special Constables based at Eltham Police Station with support at other times provided by 'Specials' from Lee Road and Westcombe Park Police Stations. Observers standing at the top of Severndroog Castle had a telephone connection to a Central Observation Station.[69]

ABOVE RIGHT: A cap badge worn by London's Metropolitan Police Special Constables during the First World War. The force of volunteer policemen, raised under the Special Constables Act of 1914, assisted greatly in policing the capital during the war years.

BELOW: The view from the top of Severndroog Castle looking towards the centre of a mist-shrouded London.

On the night of 24/25 August 1916, Severndroog Castle had a narrow escape. Heinrich Mathy, commanding Zeppelin L 31, had approached London unobserved and commenced dropping his bombs over the Isle of Dogs and Deptford, before following a course across south-east London. No searchlights picked up L 31 until it reached Shooter's Hill. The Zeppelin passed directly over Severndroog Castle, dropping two high-explosive bombs that exploded just to the east of it. Fragments of the bomb struck the tower but 'no great damage was done … The Special Constables coolly stuck to their work, and continued faithfully to telephone the results of their scrutiny'.

The local council closed and boarded up Severndroog Castle in 1986. It reopened to the public in 2014, after the long-term efforts of a local group formed in 2002 – The Severndroog Castle Building Preservation Trust. It is now possible to climb to the top of the castle once more for a First World War observer's view across London.

A raid relic from the Well Hall Estate

Just before L 31 dropped the bombs close to Severndroog Castle, her commander, Heinrich Mathy, released five bombs over Eltham in the area known as the Well Hall Estate, houses built in 1915 to provide accommodation for the rapidly expanding workforce at Woolwich Arsenal. One bomb, dropping In Well Hall Road, demolished one house and severely damaged those either side, killing four people inside. Another bomb, exploding in the roadway opposite No. 23 Dickson Road, smashed a gas main, damaged 21 houses and injured two men, four women, and a child, but only one needed hospital treatment. A piece of the gutter from No. 24 Dickson Road, pierced by a bomb fragment, has survived from this raid and is in a private collection.

A piece of gutter from the house at No. 24 Dickson Road, one of those damaged by the bomb that exploded in the street, and kept as a souvenir. (Courtesy of The Aero Conservancy)

54

Spähkorb or Sub-Cloud Car

An eye in the sky

The idea behind the development of the *Spähkorb* (spy basket) or sub-cloud car as it was known by the British, is given by Army airship captain, Ernst Lehmann, in his book *The Zeppelins*:

'Our idea was to produce a small observation car which might be lowered a half a mile or more below the Zeppelin. In that an observer could ride and direct the course and the firing [by telephone], while the big ship floated serenely above him in a cloud bank or mist.'[70]

Lehmann did not come up with the original idea, but he did design one that Zeppelin Z XII used effectively in action over Calais on 17 March 1915; a newspaper reporting that the Zeppelin 'made a systematic tour of important points'. Although a number of Army Zeppelins carried a *Spähkorb*, the Naval Airship Division never embraced the idea. That may have had something to do with the fact that during a trial the commander of the Division, Peter Strasser, was in one when the cable became entangled, turning the car upside down and leaving him hanging on for his life 300 feet below the Zeppelin!

During the largest airship raid of the war, on the night of 2/3 September 1916, Army Zeppelin LZ 90 appeared over Essex. She encountered problems with the winch, which began to run free, allowing her *Spähkorb* to drop uncontrollably. Hovering over the parish of Mistley, the crew of LZ 90 tried to recover the situation, stopping the winch by thrusting a metal bar into the teeth of the gear-wheels.

The *Spähkorb* or sub-cloud car dropped by Army Zeppelin LZ 90 over Essex during the raid of 2/3 September 1916.

Unable to recover the *Spähkorb*, the crew restarted the engines, cut its cable and moved off. At that point a local man heard what he described as 'the thud of a falling body'. About an hour later the crew jettisoned the now useless winch as they passed over Poslingford in Suffolk. The following morning the bailiff at Abbott's Hall Farm near Horsley Cross discovered the *Spähkorb* lying in the field with several hundred yards of cable trailing along the ground.[71]

After the authorities had made a complete study of the *Spähkorb*, which measured just over 14 feet in length, it went on exhibition in September and October with other Zeppelin relics to raise money for charitable causes, chiefly the Red Cross. Later it became part of the Imperial War Museum collection.

ABOVE RIGHT: The jettisoned *Spähkorb* fascinated the British public. This image made the front cover of *The Sphere*, an illustrated newspaper, on 14 October 1916, and shows an observer inside through a cutaway section.

BELOW: LZ 90's *Spähkorb* went on display at the Honourable Artillery Company's London headquarters on 26 September 1916, initially with relics from the crash site of Schütte-Lanz SL 11 and later with wreckage from Zeppelin L 32.

55

H. Scott Orr's 'Destruction of a Zeppelin'

An artistic version of the last moments of Schütte-Lanz SL 11

In the early hours of Sunday, 3 September 1916, Lieutenant William Leefe Robinson, flying a B.E.2c of No. 39 Home Defence Squadron, appeared out of the darkness and pounced on a German airship over Hertfordshire to the north of London. Fierce anti-aircraft fire had already turned the raider away from London, but the effects of the bombs dropped by the wooden-framed Schütte-Lanz, SL 11, now drew Robinson to the scene.

On the third attack his incendiary and explosive bullets succeeded in igniting the hydrogen in the colossal airship. Now burning and falling, the airship – a flaring, flaming wreck – smashed into a field at the village of Cuffley. Hundreds of thousands of Londoners, and many more people across the counties surrounding the capital, had been staring skywards, transfixed, as the combat reached its climax. Among them was a photographer, H. Scott Orr, who had his studio at Woodford Green, about nine miles from Cuffley.

Recognising the significance of the moment, Scott Orr created a series of six tinted gelatin silver prints in his studio illustrating the demise of SL 11, marked as 'First Position' through to 'Sixth Position'. These were not photographs, rather they were images created in the studio reflecting what Scott Orr saw as SL 11 fell to earth. He sold them under the title, 'The Morning of Third September, 1916, Destruction of Zeppelin near London', with the Press Bureau sanctioning their issue. A close inspection of the first picture shows that Scott Orr based his airship image on a pre-war Zeppelin type; it bears no resemblance to the layout of a Schütte-Lanz airship. Clearly H. Scott Orr produced the prints quickly because William Leefe Robinson wrote to him a month later thanking him for the 'really magnificent pictures you sent me some time ago'. He went on to say, 'They are certainly some of the best and most artistic pictures of the subject that I have seen,' and ordered three more sets.[72]

The pictures were also produced as a set of six postcards aimed at the mass market, with each image given a time from 2.05am to 2.25am and titles such as 'Danger Ahead', 'Airman Attacks' and 'Nearing the End'. The public demand for such souvenirs was enormous. It was as though the threat from the German airships, under which the British public had lived since the war began, had melted away in that blinding flare of burning hydrogen.

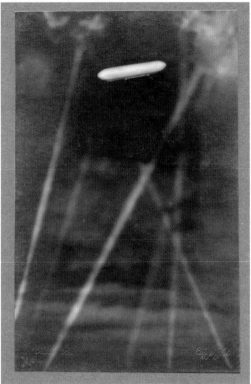
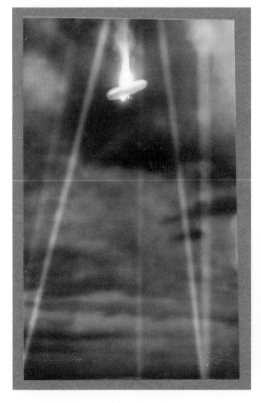
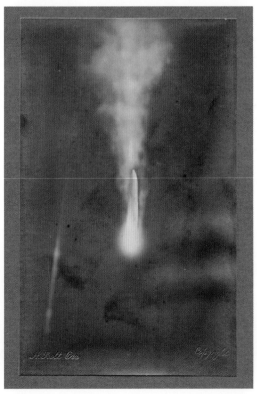

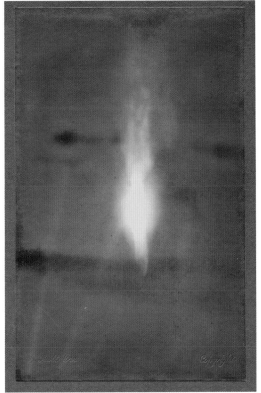 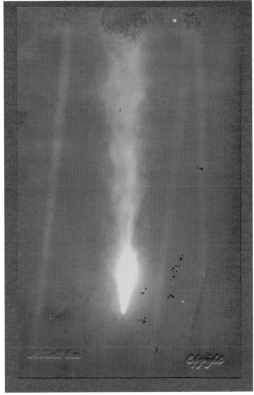

ABOVE and OPPOSITE: A set of the six gelatin silver prints produced in the Woodford Green studio of H. Scott Orr. He called the series 'Destruction of Zeppelin near London'.

RIGHT: An original folder that protected the set of prints when they went on sale. (Courtesy of Department of Special Collections, McFarlin Library, University of Tulsa)

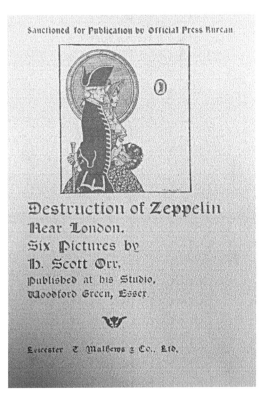

The back of each of the six prints bore the simple description 'First Position' through to 'Sixth Position' and the words 'Sanctioned by the Press Bureau'. (Courtesy of Department of Special Collections, McFarlin Library, University of Tulsa)

H. SCOTT ORR,
THE STUDIO,
HIGH ROAD,
WOODFORD GREEN.

SANCTIONED BY OFFICIAL PRESS BUREAU.

3-SEP1916

FIRST POSITION

Sanctioned by Official Press Bureau.   **AIRMAN ATTACKS.**   Copyright. H. Scott Orr.
About 2-18 a.m. Sunday, Sept. 3rd, 1916.

The images were also released as a set of six postcards for the mass market and one is shown here. This is the third card in the series, as SL 11 begins to burn; it is titled 'Airman Attacks', with a time given of 2.18am.

56

The Cuffley Red Cross Souvenirs

How to dispose of three tons of German wire

The destruction of SL 11 at Cuffley in Hertfordshire was a momentous event in the history of the First Blitz. Although not the first airship shot down, it was the first over mainland Britain, with its demise witnessed by countless thousands of ordinary people. The following day many made a pilgrimage out to the crash site, to see where one of the hated German airships had met its end and maybe to find a souvenir. As most of the wooden structure of the Schütte-Lanz disappeared in the raging fire, what they saw in abundance was wire, vast quantities of which braced the airship. Salvage parties rolled it up into huge bundles, but what to do with it next? Happily there was a solution at hand; the War Office gave three tons of it to the Red Cross Society.

Thursday, 19 October 1916 had been set aside as 'Our Day', a flag day organised by the Joint Committee of the Red Cross Society and the Order of St John to raise money for the care of sick and wounded members of the armed forces. On 28 September an announcement stated that the donated wire was to be 'manufactured into rings, bracelets, charms and other articles', for sale to the public.[73] Concerned, however, that not enough souvenirs would be ready in time, a decision was taken to just cut up much of the wire into small pieces and place them in special envelopes 'which will be the guarantee of the Red Cross Society that the specimen is a genuine portion of the wrecked airship'.[74]

Wounded soldiers cut up the strips of wire, while 14 firms in London, Birmingham,

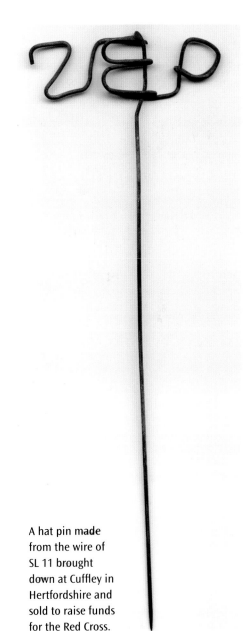

A hat pin made from the wire of SL 11 brought down at Cuffley in Hertfordshire and sold to raise funds for the Red Cross.

Sheffield and Manchester turned the rest into other items, as indicated on a price list published on 5 October: 'Short length of wire in official envelope, 1s.: safety-pin brooch, 2s.6d.: fancy brooch, 5s.: ring, 10s.6d.: hatpin, 10s.6d.: cuff-links, 1 guinea: bracelet, 1 guinea.'[75]

Despite all these efforts, the demand for the souvenirs outstripped supply.

'Of the million strips of wire from the wreck of the Cuffley raider, London had half a million for her share, and very soon they were all sold. Meanwhile Lady Derby at Liverpool and many others in other parts of the country were disposing of the remaining half-million.'

The delighted organiser of 'Our Day', May Beeman, was happy to describe the Cuffley airship as 'the Kaiser's gift to the Red Cross'.

A Red Cross envelope containing a small piece of wire from SL 11. This simple and quick to produce souvenir was made available when doubts arose as to whether enough of the original more elaborate souvenirs would be ready for sale by 'Our Day' on 19 October 1916. (The David Marks Collection)

A piece of wire from SL 11 twisted to form the word 'ZEP' and sold for 1s, raising funds for the Red Cross. (The David Marks Collection)

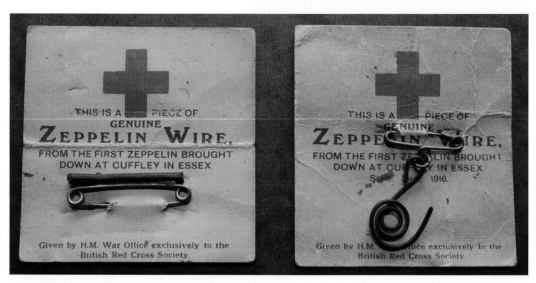

Two 'Cuffley' wire souvenirs. On the left a simple piece of wire soldered to a pin brooch, and on the right a more elaborate hanging design. These souvenirs proved highly popular; reports claim a million were sold in October 1916. (The David Marks Collection)

57

The Church of St Mary the Virgin
Essendon, Hertfordshire

The impact of a raid on a quiet rural village

While SL 11 attempted to reach London on the night of 2/3 September 1916, other German airships were also on the outskirts of the capital. One of them, Zeppelin L 16, commanded by Kapitänleutnant Erich Sommerfeldt, arrived over Potters Bar, Hertfordshire, at 2.15am as SL 11 struggled to free itself from the probing searchlights and rapidly firing AA guns. Sommerfeldt turned his attention to a searchlight sweeping the sky about five miles away at the village of Essendon. At 2.20am he circled over the village, where the sound of the Zeppelin's engines awoke 26-year-old Frances Bamford, who worked as a telephonist at the Hatfield telephone exchange. Realising the local searchlight was in action, she awoke her father, who roused the family. Frances told him that she would go into work as she imagined the night staff may need help, but before she could do so a bomb exploded nearby. Mr Bamford ordered his family out of the house, where they scattered into a paddock. It was an unfortunate choice; the house was untouched by the bombs but out in the field a fragment from one killed Frances, and her 12-year-old sister Eleanor died from her injuries.[76]

Another bomb struck the local church of St Mary the Virgin. It exploded on the roof of the vestry, smashing the ceiling above the altar, blasting a hole in the south wall of the chancel, wrecking the organ and smashing the windows.

Moments after the bombs dropped, the crew of L 16 could only look on as SL 11 burst into flames over the village of Cuffley. With the intense flare of light from the burning airship now illuminating the great bulk of L 16, Sommerfeldt steered away and set course for home.

Three days later the funeral of the two sisters took place in the damaged church, after which they were buried together in the churchyard.

Financed by an insurance claim, repairs to the church soon began and exactly one year later the restoration was complete, a plaque to commemorate the occasion built into the outside wall of the rebuilt section. It bears the words: 'In devout thanksgiving to Almighty God this stone is placed here in commemoration of the reopening on Sunday, 2 September 1917 of this chancel, vestry and organ chamber after the rebuilding necessitated by a Zeppelin raid on Sunday, 3 September 1916.'

The section of the Church of St Mary the Virgin at Essendon damaged by a bomb dropped by Zeppelin L 16. (Courtesy of Mark Lawley)

ABOVE LEFT: The plaque on the church commemorating completion of the restoration work exactly a year after the raid. (Courtesy of Mark Lawley)

ABOVE RIGHT: The grave of the Bamford sisters, Frances and Eleanor, in the churchyard; both were killed by a bomb dropped from L 16. (Courtesy of Mark Lawley)

A close-up of the inscription on the grave of the Bamford sisters. (Courtesy of Mark Lawley)

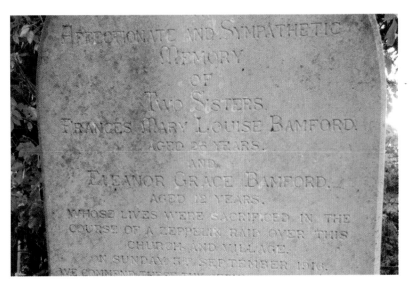

58

Souvenir Matchbox Cover

In that moment in the early hours of Sunday, 3 September 1916, when William Leefe Robinson pounced on German airship SL 11 and shot it down over Cuffley in Hertfordshire, his own life changed forever.

Robinson's attack was preceded by an intense bombardment from the AA guns defending London, which drew countless thousands of people out onto the streets and into their gardens to watch this extraordinary spectacle in the sky. When Robinson's bullets did their work and SL 11 burst into a flaming inferno, wild cheers broke out across the city as people danced in celebration and parents dragged their children from their beds to witness the sight of the hated airship plummeting to earth. That blinding flash of burning hydrogen destroyed in an instant the illusion of invincibility German airships had enjoyed since the first raid in January 1915.

William Leefe Robinson, feted and mobbed wherever he went, became an instant celebrity as the first man to shoot down a German airship over British soil. At a time when the newspapers had little to publish but bad news, such as the endless casualty lists from the Battle of the Somme, here was a tonic for the British public. Newspapers filled their pages with stories of Robinson's thrilling deed and, keen to capitalise on this 'good news' story, two

days later it was announced that Robinson was to receive the Victoria Cross 'for most conspicuous bravery', one of the fastest awards in the medal's

One of the souvenirs made to cash in on the popularity of Robinson – a matchbox holder bearing his picture. (Courtesy of David Marks)

history. He received his medal from the King at Windsor Castle on 9 September.

Robinson, a quiet, modest hero, received a significant amount of cash as 'prize money', donated by a number of wealthy industrialists and businessmen, which had been on offer for the first person to bring down an enemy airship over Britain. He received the sum of £4,250, which, incredibly, would be worth well over £300,000 today. Robinson's face began to appear everywhere, in newspapers, magazines, on postcards, and commemorative items such as matchbox covers, biscuit tins and the like. Much to his frustration, however, the authorities grounded him, unwilling to lose such a valuable asset, and instead sent him around the country on numerous official engagements. William Leefe Robinson had arguably become the most famous soldier in the British Army, his fame enduring to this day.

ABOVE: William Leefe Robinson adorns the front cover of *The Great War* magazine dated 27 January 1917. The magazine began publishing a weekly edition at the beginning of the war, keeping up with events across the globe right until the end.

BELOW: William Leefe Robinson cheered by men of the Royal Flying Corps after the announcement of the award of the Victoria Cross.

'Going! Going!! Gone!!! – The man behind the gun'.
One of the many souvenir postcards celebrating
Robinson's deed in shooting down SL 11.

Another dramatic souvenir card commemorating
Robinson's destruction of a German airship. The card
states, as was common at the time, that his victim
was Zeppelin L 21. The authorities were happy to go
along with this, not wanting to lessen the impact by
announcing it was not one of the hated Zeppelins
Robinson had shot down, but rather a Schütte-Lanz,
which few in Britain had heard of.

Tribute to a hero

While the excitement over the destruction of SL 11 filled the pages of Britain's newspapers, on 6 September 1916 the *Daily Express* reported that Mrs J. M. B. Kidston of Nyn Park, Northaw, the owner of the ground where the airship came to earth, was 'happy to donate land for a monument'. In response, the *Daily Express* invited its readers to subscribe to a fund to erect a memorial to commemorate William Leefe Robinson's deed. But before it was ready, Robinson was dead.

Grounded after his exploits, and spending his time attending official engagements, Robinson yearned to return to active service. He eventually got his way with a posting to No. 48 Squadron, which was preparing for service in France. The squadron made its first operational flight on 5 April 1917, with Robinson leading a flight of six Bristol F.2A 'Bristol Fighters'. It did not end well. Attacked by Manfred von Richthofen's *Jagdstaffel* 11, Robinson's flight lost four aircraft. Robinson made a forced landing near Douai and remained a PoW for the rest of the war.

Robinson proved a determined but unsuccessful escapee, and with his name already known in Germany after the destruction of SL 11, he found himself on the receiving end of harsh treatment at the notorious Holzminden camp. He arrived back in England in December 1918 but just

The William Leefe Robinson memorial at Cuffley in Hertfordshire. Readers of the *Daily Express* newspaper funded the memorial; they had previously funded a memorial to Reginald Warneford in Brompton cemetery (see Object 14).

ABOVE LEFT: Robinson's VC citation on one of the memorial's flanking panels.

ABOVE RIGHT: William Leefe Robinson's grave in All Saints Church cemetery extension in Harrow Weald.

17 days later a much-weakened William Leefe Robinson succumbed to the influenza pandemic sweeping the planet and died on 31 December. Buried on 3 January 1919, a crowd of thousands attended as he was laid to rest in the cemetery of All Saints Church, Harrow Weald.

The work on the Cuffley memorial continued and at its unveiling in June 1921, it carried the dedication: 'Erected by readers of the 'Daily Express' to the memory of Captain William Leefe Robinson, VC.'

It is worth noting that the original inscription on the memorial referred to the destruction of L 21 and only in 1966 was it corrected to SL 11. At the time the authorities considered it advantageous to public morale to maintain the belief that the victim was a Zeppelin – hence L 21, another of that night's raiders – and not a rival type made by Schütte-Lanz. An inscription on William Leefe Robinson's grave still refers to L 21.

59

Silver Watch – Little Wigborough, Essex

A reward for the arrest of the crew of Zeppelin L 33

The loss of the Army's SL 11 did not deter the Naval Airship Division from continuing their attacks on Britain, and on 23 September 1916 they launched a 12-Zeppelin raid. Two turned back early with engine problems and a third did not come inland, but the other nine dropped bombs over a wide area of England, across London, Kent, Surrey, Essex, Suffolk, Lincolnshire, Nottinghamshire and East Yorkshire. For Zeppelin L 33, only commissioned on 2 September, it was to be its first – and last – raid.

Commanded by Kapitänleutnant Alois Böcker, L 33 had reached the eastern districts of London and begun dropping bombs when struck by a shell fired from an anti-aircraft gun. It destroyed one gas cell, while fragments slashed through others and fractured one of the main structural rings between the control gondola and midships engine gondolas. Fortunately for the crew, the escaping hydrogen did not ignite, but L 33 was in trouble. It managed to brush off an attack made by 2nd Lieutenant Alfred de Bathe Brandon, No. 39 Squadron RFC, but was now losing height (see Object 44). Böcker ordered the crew to jettison everything they could to slow their descent, hoping to limp home, but it was to no avail. L 33 hit the ground in a field at Little Wigborough in Essex. Despite their best efforts, the crew failed to destroy their airship by fire. Unable to do anymore, Böcker formed his men and marched away; 21 German servicemen were now at large in the British countryside.

There had been plenty of stories in the British press of the activities of the 'beastly Hun' to cause concern for those in the locality. Those living nearest to the crash site hid in their houses, but not Special Constable Edgar Nicholas.

Nicholas, awoken by an explosion from L 33, had looked out of his window and saw a fire burning in the distance. He quickly dressed, grabbed his bicycle and pedalled towards it. As he cycled along the Wigborough Road, he encountered Kapitänleutnant Alois Böcker and his men coming towards him. The extremely cool Nicholas dismounted, walked up to the group and shone his torch on Böcker, asking him, 'Is it a Zeppelin down?' The German commander ignored the question then enquired in English, 'How many miles is it to Colchester?' Nicholas told him it was about six miles, for which Böcker thanked him. By now Nicholas understood the situation: 'I at once recognised a foreign accent and from their clothing and conversation knew they were Germans.'[77]

Böcker abandoned any fleeting ideas he may have had of trying to escape and the extraordinary assembly set off together along the road leading to the village of Peldon, where there was a Post Office, a telephone and the local police constable, Charles Smith. Joined on the way by another 'Special' and a police sergeant holidaying in the area, the three men handed over the captured crew to Smith, who formally arrested them. Smith received instructions to march towards West Mersea, from where a military escort would meet him on the road. Edgar Nicholas went back to the site of the crashed Zeppelin to watch over it, leaving PC Smith and seven 'Specials' to escort the crew of L 33 into captivity.

At the end of September a fund was set up to purchase watches for the Special Constables and others who had played a part in the capture of the crew of L 33. These silver half-hunter watches were presented at a special ceremony on 2 December 1916 and bore the inscription: ESSEX CONSTABULARY – PRESENTED TO (Name) FOR GOOD SERVICES WHEN ZEPPELIN L.33 WAS BROUGHT DOWN IN ESSEX ON 24.9.16. Some are still the prized possessions of their families.

The silver watch presented to Special Constable Thomas Wyncoll for his 'good services' on the night Zeppelin L 33 came down at Little Wigborough in Essex. (Courtesy of Geoffrey Wyncoll)

ABOVE: The inscription on Thomas Wyncoll's watch. Each watch bore an identical inscription, with just the name changed. (Courtesy of Geoffrey Wyncoll)

RIGHT: The watch presented to Special Constable Clement Hyam still in its original presentation box. (Courtesy of the owner, who wishes to remain anonymous)

BELOW: A postcard showing the Special Constables involved in escorting the crew of L 33. Edgar Nicholas stands in the doorway while Thomas Wyncoll is sitting on the wall second from the right and Clem Hyam is believed to be the one nearest the camera. (The David Marks Collection)

The Eight Essex Special Constables who arrested Zeppelin Crew, September 24th. *1916.*

A souvenir from the crew of Zeppelin L 33

The entire crew of L 33 walked away from the wreck of their Zeppelin. They were understandably happy to have landed safely and not shot down in flames. Special Constable Nicholas reported how one of the crew was particularly chatty as he escorted them towards Peldon and handed him personal items as souvenirs. It seems others behaved similarly to those they encountered before they were handed over to the military. A naval cap (*matrosenmütze*) from one of the crew is now in the collection of the Imperial War Museum, as are badges and insignia removed from the sleeves of the crew's uniforms. The owner of the cap may have been close to the explosion or fire when L 33 landed as there is evidence of burning on the right-hand side. Whether it fell overboard or was given or taken as a souvenir is unrecorded.

A German *Matrosenmütze* belonging to one of the crew of L 33. Whether it was dropped or handed over as a souvenir by a crewman happy to be alive after the Zeppelin came down is unknown.

THE CREW OF ZEPPELIN L33, TWENTY TWO IN NUMBER, BROUGHT DOWN ON THE ESSEX COAST DURING THE EARLY HOURS OF SUNDAY, SEPT. 24TH, 1916. A SPECIAL CONSTABLE APPEARED ON THE SCENE, AND IN THE WORDS OF A LOCAL RUSTIC—"HE TOOK UP THE WHOLE OF 'EM."

This postcard shows Special Constable Edgar Nicholas escorting the crew of L 33 towards the village of Peldon, although in reality he took up a position at the rear of the column. At Peldon, Police Constable Charles Smith arrested the crew.

60

Zeppelin Souvenirs – Essex

Mementoes from the crash sites of Zeppelins L 32 and L 33

When two Zeppelins came down in Essex on the night of 23/24 September 1916, there was a huge demand for souvenirs from the wreckage, yet taking things was frowned upon by the authorities. Keen to analyse all items recovered from Zeppelin wrecks, the military were quick to erect cordons around crash sites. But often the local population would arrive before the police or the military and grabbed mementoes before it was too late. After the authorities had completed initial inspections, war charities often received parts of the wreckage to sell on to raise funds. More skilled individuals could melt down sections of the duralumin

BELOW and OVERLEAF: A selection of souvenirs made from the wreckage of Zeppelin L 32. The piece below shows L 32 breaking in half as flames burst forth from the centre of the Zeppelin. On the following page pieces of duralumin have been fashioned into a pocket watch holder, a British biplane and L 32 in full profile.

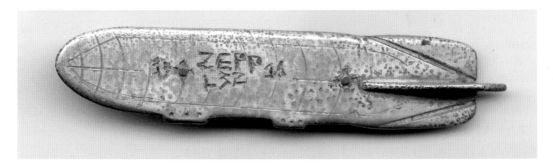

structure and cast them into collectable souvenirs. Smaller items such as crosses, napkin rings and brooches, formed from pieces of duralumin and stamped with the Zeppelin's service number, proved popular. Fragments of the framework or scraps of the linen envelope were also prized. A large section of a girder from L 33 was given to Little Wigborough's church, St Nicholas, which stands about 500 yards from the crash site. In the case of L33, the unexpected gift of a complete Zeppelin framework meant the authorities spent much time examining her structure, but the wreckage of L 32, shot down over Billericay, offered less of value. Ten days later, parts of the wreckage of this latter Zeppelin were on display in London alongside items from SL 11, shot down at Cuffley in Hertfordshire.

Those people who did help themselves to souvenirs were in contravention of Section 35B of the Defence of the Realm Regulations and could find themselves in court. Despite the penalties, however, many were prepared to take the risk and there are reports of soldiers manning the cordons around crash sites selling pieces to earn a little money. When the real items ran out, they could always sell a piece of old scrap metal to the unwary customer – a practice that is sometimes evident on online auction sites today! After the crashes of L 32 and L 33, the Essex Police were vigorous in their pursuit of local people whom they believed had articles in their possession. Even so, the great variety of souvenir items that still exist would appear to indicate they were not always successful.

This selection of souvenirs were created from the remains of L 33. Clockwise from top right: a small section of duralumin girder, a napkin ring, a section of flattened radiator pipe, a piece of fabric taken from L 33's envelope with what appears to be a bullet hole showing charred edges and a small cross stamped with L 33.

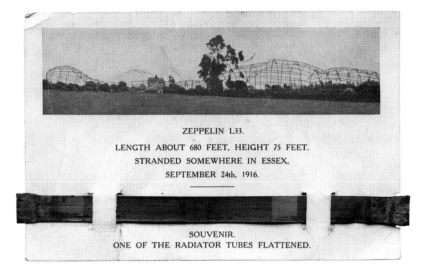

ZEPPELIN L33.
LENGTH ABOUT 680 FEET, HEIGHT 75 FEET.
STRANDED SOMEWHERE IN ESSEX,
SEPTEMBER 24th, 1916.

SOUVENIR.
ONE OF THE RADIATOR TUBES FLATTENED.

61

The Windows of St John's Church Washingborough, Lincolnshire

'A lasting thanksgiving that no one was hurt'

While the careers of Zeppelins L 32 and L 33 ended in Essex on the night of 23/24 September 1916, the other seven raiders all returned home safely having met with mixed results over England.

One of them, Zeppelin L 14, came inland over Skegness on the Lincolnshire coast then steered a course towards Lincoln. A searchlight positioned at Washingborough, about three miles east of Lincoln, fixed on the raider and an AA gun at Canwick opened fire. This reaction appears to have convinced Kuno Manger, the commander of L 14, that he had reached Lincoln and in response he released his entire bomb load, which fell around the villages of Heighington, Washingborough and Greetwell. At Washingborough 12 high-explosive bombs fell in fields, where they dug craters, uprooted an orchard, destroyed a chicken house and damaged some outbuildings, but no one was injured. The village had escaped lightly, much to the relief of the rector at St John's Church, the Rev. William Burland.

Burland was an interesting character. His family considered him a 'rather reluctant parson'.

One of eight identical stained glass windows in the church at Washingborough, installed as a 'lasting thanksgiving that no one was hurt' in the Zeppelin raid. The windows all feature the service numbers of Zeppelins L 30 and L 32. (Courtesy of Mark Lawley)

St John's Church in Washingborough. The distinct shapes of four of the eight Zeppelin windows are visible to the left of the church tower.

His sermons, it seems, 'made little sense', and 'he would have the church bells rung to let the Bishop of Lincoln think he was having a service whilst he was off hunting'.[78] To mark the village's safe delivery from the bombs, and as a 'lasting thanksgiving that no one was hurt', the Rev. Burland had eight identical stained glass windows installed in the church. The design he chose, though, was unusual. Each window features the service number of the same two Zeppelins: L 30 and L 32 and the letters ZZ. Neither of these two Zeppelins had threatened Lincolnshire. However, that same night, Zeppelins L 32 and L 33 were brought down in Essex. The service numbers of both these appeared in the press and it may simply be that Burland decided to combine the destruction of these two Zeppelins with the safe delivery of the village, but mistakenly confused L 33 with another Zeppelin, L 30.

The Zeppelin Memorial windows are in the clerestory of the nave, along both sides of the church.

62

Silver 'Zeppelin' Cup – Hornchurch, Essex
A village expresses its gratitude

The exploits of William Leefe Robinson, of No. 39 Squadron, in shooting down SL 11 in the early hours of 3 September 1916 became a matter of local pride for the residents of Hornchurch in Essex. Sutton's Farm, the airfield from which Robinson had flown that night, lay just south of the village.

As a mark of their admiration, the parish council announced a fund to purchase a gift for Robinson. Between 2,000 and 3,000 people enthusiastically made donations of between 1d and 2s 6d, but before the purchase of a gift another pilot from the squadron, Frederick Sowrey, shot down Zeppelin L 32. While the organising committee pondered what to do, Robinson solved the problem for them. He wrote to W. H. Legg, Chairman of the Parish Council: 'Since Lieutenant Sowrey has performed a similar deed, I wish him to equally share your gift, whatever it may be.' The parish council went ahead and purchased two handsome silver cups, which they had engraved. But then, just a week after Sowrey shot down L 32, Wulstan Tempest, also of No. 39 Squadron, shot down Zeppelin L 31. The council quickly purchased a third cup in time for the presentation set for Saturday, 14 October 1916, in the grounds of Grey Towers, Hornchurch, site of the New Zealand Convalescent Hospital.[79] On the day only Robinson and Sowrey were able to attend, Tempest was on duty. Robinson accepted his own cup and Tempest's, making a short speech. He remarked that he had received many gifts to mark his achievement, but few

The silver cup presented to Frederick Sowrey by the residents of Hornchurch 'as a token of admiration and gratitude' after he shot down Zeppelin L 32 in September 1916.

ABOVE: The recipients of the Hornchurch silver cups: William Leefe Robinson, Wulstan Tempest and Frederick Sowrey.

RIGHT: Robinson accepting his cup at the presentation held in a marquee at Grey Towers, Hornchurch, on 14 October 1916. Sowrey is sitting second from the right. (The David Marks Collection)

Presentation of cups to the three Zeppelin heroes, by residents of an Essex village. Captain L. W. Robinson, V.C., receiving his cup.

he would appreciate more. Considering he had already received his Victoria Cross and cash rewards amounting to £4,250 (worth over £300,000 today), it is clear that Robinson was a master in the art of diplomacy. When Sowrey accepted his cup he declined to make a speech, he simply said he was deeply grateful.

The cup shown here is that presented to Frederick Sowrey and which remains with the family. The wording on each cup was similar.

In this instance it says: 'Presented by the residents of Hornchurch, Essex, as a token of admiration and gratitude – Second Lieutenant Frederick Sowrey, D.S.O. Royal Fusiliers and Royal Flying Corps – When stationed at the Hornchurch aerodrome Second Lieutenant Sowrey with great gallantry attacked and destroyed an enemy airship under circumstances of great difficulty and danger during the night of September 23–24 1916.'

63

A Zeppelin Victim
Holcombe, Lancashire

A dead thrush – the lone victim of a raid

Less than two days after the loss of L 32 and L 33, Peter Strasser, head of Germany's Naval Airship Division, ordered another raid. Six Zeppelins set out on 25 September 1916, with four targeting the north of England and industrial Midlands. One of them, L 21, commanded by Oberleutnant-zur-See Kurt Frankenburg, passed over the Peak District and Pennines into Lancashire.

The first bombs fell at Newchurch, Rawtenstall, Ewood Bridge and Lumb, before L 21 approached the village of Holcombe, about six miles north-east of Bolton. Here, Frankenburg released five high-explosive bombs.

The unfortunate thrush, the only victim of the raid on Holcombe in Lancashire, carried out by Zeppelin L 21, the same Zeppelin that the press had reported shot down at Cuffley three weeks earlier. (Courtesy of Sue Wardle, Emmanuel Holcombe School)

Gouges in the stonework of the building that was once the Post Office in Holcombe, caused by one of the bombs dropped by L 21. (Courtesy of Sue Wardle, Emmanuel Holcombe School)

A group of local men speaking to a newspaper reporter described the sound of the approaching Zeppelin 'like that of a traction engine'. One of the men continued, 'Then five or six shells exploded almost all at once. It was like thunder. And then you could hear the windows smashing everywhere. The concussion did the damage.'[80]

The blast from two bombs that exploded in a field close to the village school stopped the clock in the tower of the village church and smashed windows there. These bombs also toppled a stout field wall, 'scattering the big stones ... like chaff', and smashed windows at the school. One bomb fragment flew with such force that it pierced right through the six-inch thick outer wall of the school. It is still possible to see blast marks on the gable end of the building.

Damage caused by another bomb, however, is easier to see. It exploded in the roadway between the Shoulder of Mutton Inn and the building opposite, which at the time was the village post office. The reporter wrote that the bomb, 'played havoc with [the] village post office, breaking woodwork and glass, and deeply pitting all the stonework to a height of about nine feet'. Some of that damage to the building remains clearly visible. The blast from that bomb also smashed about 20 windows at the inn, where there was also a farm, which suffered significant damage to a barn and cow shed.

There was only one official casualty in Holcombe. One of the bombs near the school killed a thrush, blasting it from its roost. To mark the raid on their village the school had the lone victim stuffed and placed in a glass case – it now appears on the War Memorials Register maintained by the Imperial War Museum.

64

A Child's Sewing Cards
Sheffield, South Yorkshire
Scattered playthings among the wreckage

On the night of 25/26 September 1916, six Zeppelins appeared over the Midlands and industrial North of England. One of these raiders, Kapitänleutnant Martin Dietrich's L 22, crossed Lincolnshire and into Yorkshire before heading towards the city of Sheffield. Some 30 bombs fell on the city, and although a number landed close to important industrial centres, most actually fell among workers' homes. Two bombs that exploded in Cossey Road, in the shadow of the huge Atlas Steel & Iron Works, had a devastating impact.

The city had air raid warning 'buzzers' and these sounded to warn Sheffield's population of a possible attack. Officially the advice in these

ABOVE and OPPOSITE: Two of the four sewing cards recovered from the wreckage of the houses destroyed by a Zeppelin bomb in Cossey Road, Sheffield. Only one had been completed. (Courtesy of Europeana 1914–1918)

circumstances was to seek shelter in a cellar. Accordingly, two families in Cossey Road did just that with William and Sarah Southerington from No. 24 joining their neighbours at No. 26, the home of George and Eliza Harrison, their 12-year-old daughter Vera, as well as their married daughter, Nellie Rhodes, with her two young children, Phyllis and Elsie. George Harrison and William Southerington remained talking in the living room while the others went down to the cellar. The sound of exploding bombs at about 12.30am no doubt cut their conversation short.

A high-explosive bomb released by Zeppelin L 22 streaked down to make a direct hit on No. 26 Cossey Road. It burst through the roof, smashed down through the house and exploded in the cellar. As a newspaper reported, the bomb 'blew everything to smithereens', adding that 'the work of recovering the bodies was ghastly'.[81] All

eight people in the house died. The explosion also destroyed No. 28, the house next door, home to Albert and Alice Newton. Blasted out of the house in opposite directions, Albert's lifeless body landed in the back yard while Alice lay on the pavement at the front. The bomb claimed the lives of ten people.

While the rubble still lay in the street, a girl picked up four cards from the debris of the houses and kept them along with a newspaper cutting naming those killed in the raid. The cards showed pictures of dogs, a pig and a turkey, perforated with holes as guides for sewing. Only one, the turkey, had been completed. Looking at the ages of the people in the houses wrecked by the bomb, the most likely owner would appear to be 12-year-old Vera Harrison. Perhaps she took them down to the cellar that night to take her mind off the anticipated raid. A poignant reminder of innocent lives lost.

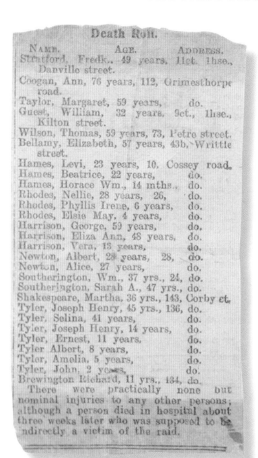

Death Roll.

NAME.	AGE.	ADDRESS.
Stratford, Fredk.,	49 years,	11ct. 1hse., Danville street.
Coogan, Ann,	76 years,	112, Grimesthorpe road.
Taylor, Margaret,	59 years,	do.
Guest, William,	32 years,	9ct., 11hse., Kilton street.
Wilson, Thomas,	59 years,	73, Petre street.
Bellamy, Elizabeth,	57 years,	43b, Writtle street.
Hames, Levi,	23 years,	10, Cossey road.
Hames, Beatrice,	22 years,	do.
Hames, Horace Wm.,	14 mths.,	do.
Rhodes, Nellie,	28 years,	26, do.
Rhodes, Phyllis Irene,	6 years,	do.
Rhodes, Elsie May,	4 years,	do.
Harrison, George,	59 years,	do.
Harrison, Eliza Ann,	48 years,	do.
Harrison, Vera,	13 years,	do.
Newton, Albert,	29 years,	28, do.
Newton, Alice,	27 years,	do.
Southerington, Wm.,	37 yrs.,	24, do.
Southerington, Sarah A.,	47 yrs.,	do.
Shakespeare, Martha,	36 yrs.,	143, Corby st.
Tyler, Joseph Henry,	45 yrs.,	136, do.
Tyler, Selina,	41 years,	do.
Tyler, Joseph Henry,	14 years,	do.
Tyler, Ernest,	11 years,	do.
Tyler Albert,	8 years,	do.
Tyler, Amelia,	5 years,	do.
Tyler, John,	2 years,	do.
Brewington Richard,	11 yrs.,	134, do.

There were practically none but nominal injuries to any other persons; although a person died in hospital about three weeks later who was supposed to be indirectly a victim of the raid.

The newspaper cutting listing those killed in the Sheffield Zeppelin raid and kept by the girl who found the sewing cards in the wrecked houses of Cossey Road. (Courtesy of Europeana 1914–1918)

Military personnel searching through the rubble of the wrecked houses in Cossey Road. The soldiers are holding up what appears to be a tablecloth, perhaps to shield the body of one of those killed in the raid. (Courtesy of Museums Sheffield)

Heinrich Mathy's Binoculars

A personal item belonging to the best known of the Zeppelin commanders

On 1 October 1916, Peter Strasser, commander of Germany's Naval Airship Division, kept up the pressure on Britain by ordering another raid on London and the Midlands. Of the 11 Zeppelins that set out, only two approached London, but neither reached the city, and this proved to be L31's final journey.

The commander of L 31, Kapitänleutnant Heinrich Mathy, was the most highly regarded of the Zeppelin captains and perhaps the only one known by name to the British public. In September 1915, after a raid on London, Mathy gave an interview to the German–American journalist Karl von Wiegand. First published in America, the interview later appeared internationally.

The bent and twisted binoculars of Heinrich Mathy, commander of L 31, who jumped to his death when his Zeppelin plummeted to earth at Potter's Bar in Hertfordshire.

For the first time the British public had an insight into the mind of a Zeppelin raider.

At 11.40pm, Zeppelin L 31 was heading towards London when the Waltham Abbey area anti-aircraft guns opened fire. In response, Mathy dropped 56 bombs as he passed over Cheshunt in Hertfordshire, enabling L 31 to climb rapidly as it headed west, attempting to evade the guns. From about 15 miles away, 2nd Lieutenant Wulstan Tempest, flying a B.E.2c, was the closest of four No. 39 Squadron pilots who saw L 31 caught in the searchlights. Tempest had a slight height advantage as he closed with L 31.

'I was flying slightly higher than the Zeppelin, and realizing that if I delayed my attack an instant longer she might climb out of my reach, I made a dive straight at her and, passing under her enormous envelope ... I put in a burst of fire from my Lewis gun.'

It had no effect. Tempest turned and now, flying in the same direction as L 31, passed under her great bulk firing a second burst, which again failed to set the Zeppelin on fire. Banking sharply, Tempest took up a position under her tail. 'I had almost begun to despair of bringing her down, when suddenly, after letting her have another burst, I saw her begin to go red inside like an immense Chinese lantern.'[82]

As the blazing, flaring wreck of L 31 plummeted down, it doomed Mathy to make a terrible choice. The quote, 'If anyone should say that he was not haunted by the visions of burning airships, then he would be a braggart,' is often attributed to him, but that is wrong. It was made after the losses sustained in September 1916 by one of his men, Pitt Klein, when crews, in sombre mood, would discuss what they would do if their time came, jump or burn to death; there were no alternatives. When his time came Heinrich Mathy jumped.[83]

A journalist writing for *The Times* visited the crash site and noted that at least two of the crew had jumped.

'So great was the force with which they struck the ground that the imprint of their frames is ... sharply defined in the grass. There is a round hole for the head, then a deep impression of the trunk with outstretched arms, and then the widely separated legs – a most uncanny sight.'[84]

Another journalist, Michael MacDonagh, gained permission to see Mathy's body. 'The only disfigurement was a slight distortion of the face. It was that of a young man, clean-shaven. He was heavily clad in a dark uniform and overcoat, with a thick muffler round his neck.'[85]

Also around Mathy's neck when he jumped were his binoculars. This battered and broken, rather poignant item, worn in action by Heinrich Mathy, now resides in the collection of the Imperial War Museum.

Kapitänleutnant Heinrich Mathy, the most highly regarded of the Zeppelin commanders, with his binoculars around his neck. Mathy was unusual amongst Zeppelin commanders in that his name was known to the public in Britain.

The propeller boss of the aircraft that shot down L 31

After his successful attack on L 31, Wulstan Tempest noted a smell of burning in the sky as: 'Far below that white-bright mass was receding, till a cloud of ascending sparks told me it had hit the ground.' Exhausted by his exertions in the freezing temperatures at high altitude, Tempest felt a 'curious calm' settle over him: 'It was a sensation I shall always remember. It was more than a sensation of relief on coming out of a bad dream; it was almost as though I came from another world.' It was with great relief that he located the flares illuminating his airfield at North Weald Bassett in Essex. Misjudging his approach, however, Tempest's B.E.2c landed badly; the undercarriage buckled and the nose dug into the earth, smashing the four-bladed propeller. Tempest hit his head painfully against his Lewis gun, but he survived the landing to receive a hero's welcome. Tempest had become the third pilot of No. 39 Squadron to shoot down a German airship.

The propeller boss of Wulstan Tempest's B.E.2c No. 4557, minus the damaged blades, is now in the collection of the RAF Museum, Hendon.

2nd Lieutenant Wulstan Tempest, No. 39 (Home Defence) Squadron, RFC. Tempest received the Distinguished Service Order for shooting down L 31 on the night of 1/2 October 1916. (The David Marks Collection)

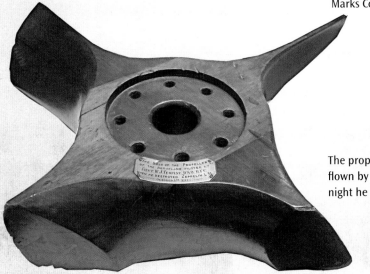

The propeller boss of the B.E.2c flown by Wulstan Tempest on the night he shot down Zeppelin L 31.

66

Zeppelin Cross
Church of St Mary the Virgin and All Saints
Potter's Bar, Hertfordshire

From weapon of war to symbol of religion

The crash of Zeppelin L 31 left around 35 tons of tangled metal wreckage littering farmland on the Oakmere Estate, Potter's Bar, held under lease by Mrs Edith Forbes. Neighbours ran to Oakmere House to alert her. Rudely awoken, she opened the door and was told excitedly what had happened. Unconcerned, Mrs Forbes replied, 'All right, we'll see to it in the morning,' and slammed the door shut again.[86] Part of the wreckage hung impaled on an oak tree in the grounds of the estate, which became known as the 'Zeppelin Oak'. This survived until the late 1930s when it was cut down as a local resident had complained of its 'rotting and dangerous condition'.

As at all the other crash sites, thousands came to see the wreckage and, if possible, obtain pieces as souvenirs. Although this was illegal, members of the public acquired many pieces of L 31's duralumin framework. One who did so was a local plumber, Mr Joyce of Southgate Road, but he did not want the pieces for himself. Mr Joyce, after some difficulty, constructed various metal frames, melted down the duralumin pieces, poured the molten metal into the framework and cast a simple but beautiful crucifix. His work completed, Mr Joyce presented the crucifix to Father George Preston at the church of St Mary the

The duralumin crucifix made of material recovered from Zeppelin L 31 and presented to the Church of St Mary the Virgin and All Saints at Potter's Bar in Hertfordshire.

Virgin and All Saints in Potter's Bar. It is said that Father Preston gratefully accepted the gift but before dedicating it he 'thoroughly purged it through immersion in Holy Water!'[87] On 3 May 1917 the new duralumin crucifix replaced the old wooden one on the altar of the All Soul's Chapel within the church. It bears an inscription in Latin, which translates as: 'To the greater glory of God and to keep alive in our memory that night of horror in which a tremendous airship threatening all with destruction by Christ's pity hurt none. This cross is dedicated by those who worship in this House of God.'

Two weeks after the installation of the new crucifix, Father Preston, who arrived in the parish in 1913, revived the old Rogation Procession in Potter's Bar, to offer a blessing to the summer crops. After a service at the church, Father Preston led the congregation out to the first station on the procession – the 'Zeppelin Oak' on the Oakmere Estate.

Father Preston leading parishioners to the 'Zeppelin Oak' in May 1917, the first station on the revived Rogation Procession.

By the 1930s the 'Zeppelin Oak' was in a dangerous condition and cut down. Housing has subsequently covered the area, but the incident is not forgotten locally; the tree stood where the black gate is now, on Wulstan Park off Tempest Avenue, named in honour of the pilot who shot down L 31.

67

'A Pledge of Love'

A relic from the wreckage of Zeppelin L 34

On 27 November 1916, following a break in an extended period of bad weather over the North Sea, the German Naval Airship Division launched a Zeppelin raid against the north-east of England and the industrial Midlands. It ended in disaster for two Zeppelin crews.

One of the raiders, Zeppelin L 34, commanded by Kapitänleutnant Max Dietrich, had come inland just north of Hartlepool at about 11.30pm. Advised of an incoming raid, 2nd Lieutenant Ian Vernon Pyott, of No. 36 Squadron, Royal Flying Corps, flying a B.E.2c, had been on patrol for just over an hour when he saw L 34 dropping bombs west of Hartlepool. Pyott attacked but his bullets had no effect. He turned on to a course parallel with the raider as it headed over West Hartlepool and commenced bombing again. Pyott attacked a second time. 'I was aiming at his port quarter and noticed first a small patch become incandescent where I had seen tracers entering his envelope … this patch rapidly spread and the next thing was that the whole Zepp was in flames.'[88]

Manning the Heugh Battery, Major S. Horsley, Durham Royal Garrison Artillery, reported that the burning wreck fell into the sea about a mile east of the battery:

'The airship remained burning for about half an hour … I then took an armed party … and proceeded to the wreck. We arrived at the scene of the wreck shortly after 1.00, but the remains had entirely disappeared, and there was nothing to be seen except a considerable amount of oil on the water.'[89]

Salvage operations commenced the following morning and divers recovered a great quantity of material from the sea, which examiners picked over once ashore at West Hartlepool.

The crude heart-shaped 'pledge of love' made from the wreckage of Zeppelin L 34 by a member of the Royal Flying Corps for his sweetheart.

ABOVE LEFT: The reverse of the 'pledge of love', confirming it was made from a small piece of L 34.

ABOVE RIGHT: While we don't know the identity of 'Jim', we do know who shot down L 34 - 2nd Lieutenant Ian Vernon Pyott of No. 36 Squadron, RFC.

There appears to be no official record of what happened to this wreckage after the experts had finished but scraps did appear as souvenirs, often attributed to the Heugh Lighthouse crew. It seems likely that both the crews of the Heugh Battery and Lighthouse managed to 'acquire' pieces of the wreckage, which they sold on to eager customers.

One small discoloured (possibly by fire) piece of duralumin from L 34 came into the possession of 'Jim', who served in the RFC. Jim worked the piece into the shape of a heart, added a small chain to allow it to be worn, then gave it to his sweetheart as 'A Pledge of Love'. Sadly, we do not know Jim's full name or whether the recipient was won over by his gesture. The fact that it has survived this long perhaps suggests she was.

68

Flt sub-Lt Gerard Fane's Flying Helmet

Personal item worn during the action that saw him awarded the DSC

The Zeppelin raid on the night of 27/28 November 1916, that saw the destruction of L 34, also marked the last raid of L 21 – the Zeppelin that had been incorrectly named at the time as the victim of William Leefe Robinson's attack on 3 September 1916. (See Object 58)

Commanded by Kapitänleutnant Kurt Frankenburg, L 21 came inland over the Yorkshire coast at 9.20pm at the beginning of an epic journey over England that lasted nine hours. Frankenburg penetrated as far west as Stoke-on-Trent before turning back eastwards. Engine problems hindered his progress, however, forcing L 21 to drift with the wind at times while mechanics worked feverishly to rectify them. At about 3am, Frankenburg skilfully evaded attacks from two aircraft of No. 38 Squadron over Lincolnshire, but this cost him valuable time. He eventually reached the coast near Great Yarmouth at about 6am but, drifting again, he headed towards Lowestoft. At 6.30am some engine power returned and L 21 headed slowly out to sea at about 35mph. A RNAS pilot flying a B.E.2c, Flight Lieutenant Egbert Cadbury, saw the airship silhouetted against the lightening dawn sky and set off in pursuit. Two other RNAS B.E.2c pilots, Flight sub-Lieutenants Edward Pulling and Gerard Fane, also gave chase.

Cadbury attacked first, firing four drums of ammunition at L 21 and coming under heavy return fire. Fane then closed in, approaching to within 100 feet of the starboard flank, but as he opened fire his Lewis gun jammed. Pulling then made his attack, closing up to 50 feet, but after just a few rounds his gun jammed too. As he turned away, however, L 21 started to burn and within a few seconds was 'nothing but a fiery furnace'.[90]

It was not entirely clear whether Cadbury or Pulling did the damage but the Navy decided to give the credit to Pulling. In an announcement made on 3 December 1916, he received the award of the Distinguished Service Order, while Cadbury and Fane both received the Distinguished Service Cross for their actions that night.

Gerard William Reginald Fane was just 18 years old. When L 21 began to burn, he looped his B.E.2c in youthful exuberance and came so close to the falling inferno at one point that the flames scorched his face and flying helmet while causing parts of his aircraft to blister. The flying helmet worn that night by Fane is now in the collection of the Fleet Air Arm Museum at Yeovilton and does appear to show some slightly scorched areas.

Flight sub-Lieutenant Gerard Fane, RNAS, took off from the air station at Burgh Castle, Norfolk, to intercept L 21, but as he lined up his attack in the icy conditions, frozen oil caused his Lewis gun to jam.

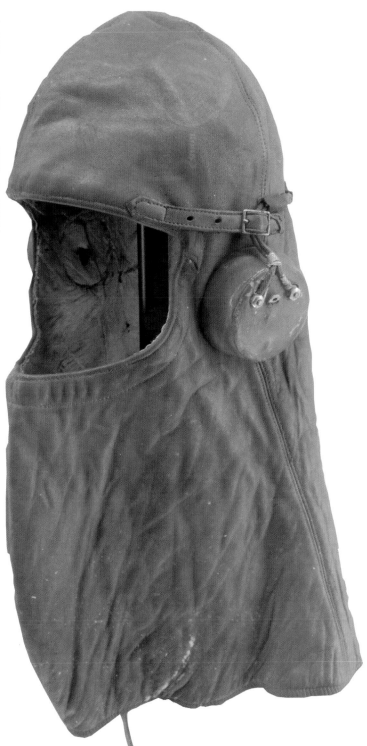

The flying helmet worn by Gerard Fane on the night he took part in the attack that destroyed Zeppelin L 21 over the North Sea. (Historic Military Press)

69

Comic Postcards

Britain discovers humour in the German air raids

When Germany first launched Zeppelin raids against Britain, one of the leading advocates, Konteradmiral Paul Behncke, Deputy Chief of the Naval Staff, expected these attacks 'to cause panic in the population which may possibly render it doubtful that the war can be continued'.

Aerial bombing, he considered, was a likely means 'of forcing England to her knees … considering the well-known nervousness of the public'.

Germany had, however, misjudged the mood of the British people. While the experience of living through an air raid was terrifying for those close to where the bombs fell, for others

ABOVE and OPPOSITE: A selection of comic postcards published during the First Blitz and which raised a smile amongst the civilian population, providing an early demonstration of the 'Blitz spirit' more commonly associated with the next World War.

further away from the danger, Zeppelin raids became something to see. People who never saw a Zeppelin could even feel cheated! Far from bringing the nation to its knees, one of the most common responses to air raids was a demand for retaliation.

Throughout the war bomb craters and damage to property became a 'must see' attraction and huge crowds would congregate around these places. Numerous picture postcards began to appear in the wake of the raids, featuring the public standing in or around bomb craters. Then, in a move that must surely have bewildered the architects of the air raids in Germany, 'comic' postcards appeared, making light of the air raids. The exact point in the history of the raids when these first appeared is unclear, but the earliest postmarks in my collection are from 1916.

These cards covered a wide variety of subjects linked with the air raids. Popular themes featured hen-pecked husbands relieved that a gas mask might silence their wives, heavy drinkers with shiny red noses contravening blackout regulations, sheltering in unusual places, young couples taking advantage of the darkness on raid nights, the effect of raids on pubs and their customers, and numerous other subjects.

Not only were these cards posted to friends and family but often they were purchased just because they raised a smile and were collected to be displayed on mantelpieces the length and breadth of the country. It was not a reaction to the air raids that Germany ever anticipated, the humour demonstrating a resilience and determination to get on with things in the face of adversity, and another early manifestation of Britain's 'Blitz spirit'. (See Object 29)

70

Stow Maries Aerodrome
Near Maldon, Essex

A WW1 home defence airfield lives again

Formed on 15 September 1916, No. 37 Squadron, RFC, was based close to the Essex coast. By the end of 1916 it had its headquarters at Woodham Mortimer and three flights: A Flight at Rochford, B Flight at Stow Maries and C Flight at Goldhanger. By August 1917, however, the squadron was concentrated at Goldhanger and Stow Maries.

The squadron first saw action on the night of 23/24 May 1917 when four Zeppelins came inland but no aircraft managed to engage. It would be the Gothas however, not the Zeppelins, that tested the pilots of No. 37 Squadron as the war progressed, with the first Gotha raid of the war launched on 25 May. Pilots based at Stow Maries, which become

An aerial view of Stow Maries, a First World War Home Defence Squadron airfield in Essex, now undergoing extensive restoration. (Courtesy of Stow Maries Great War Aerodrome)

Another aerial view of the airfield at Stow Maries showing the runways, which are now in operation, allowing aircraft to fly in and out of the site once more. (Courtesy of Stow Maries Great War Aerodrome)

home to A and B Flights, took off to oppose 24 of 27 Gotha raids.[91]

Stow Maries had been established about seven miles south-west of Maldon, on farmland to the south of Flambird's Farm, and development continued throughout the war. Not due for completion until December 1918, it appears some buildings remained unfinished when the war ended in November. A road running north–south split the site, with the flying field and hangars on the east side of the road and administrative buildings and barracks to the west. After the war all three flights of No. 37 Squadron united at Stow Maries in February

1919, but the following month the squadron relocated to Biggin Hill and the airfield closed with the land reverting to agricultural use.[92]

In more recent years, however, intensive work has begun to restore Stow Maries to its former First World War glories. Of the original buildings, 24 still exist (now Grade II Listed) and many have already benefitted from restoration, with others awaiting their turn. A museum has opened in the original squadron offices. These structures represent the largest surviving group of RFC buildings on a First World War aerodrome, which have not been adapted later for further military use. With a

A view of some of the restored First World War-era buildings at Stow Maries. The building on the left, facing the airfield, is the pilot's ready room, where aircrew on duty awaited warning of incoming raids.

restored landing field too, vintage aircraft are able to fly in and out, returning Stow Maries to a functioning airfield.

Initially saved from redevelopment by a businessman, the site has received significant funding and support in recent years. Aided by a team of dedicated volunteers, the part this airfield and the men who served here played in the story of the First Blitz will never be forgotten.

71

Tontine Street – Folkestone, Kent

The Gotha bombers arrive

While the Navy retained its faith in Zeppelins to effectively take the war to Britain after the losses sustained in the latter months of 1916, the Army switched its attention to bomber aircraft, in particular to the G-type bomber, the *Grosskampfflugzeug* (large battle aeroplane), more commonly known as the Gotha bomber.

The squadron designated for this role, *Kampfgeschwader Drei der Obersten Heeresleitung* (abbreviated to *Kagohl 3*), and popularly known as *Die Englandgeschwader* – the England Squadron – was finally ready in the spring of 1917.

The first raid aimed at London took place on 25 May 1917, but thick cloud over the capital caused the squadron to abandon their plans and return over Kent, dropping bombs across the county as they headed home. Bombs dropped by the 21 Gothas had already killed 24 people when the squadron appeared without warning over Folkestone and dropped about 40 bombs on the coastal town.

It was early Friday evening at the start of a Bank Holiday weekend. Large numbers of people were out shopping and a long queue had formed outside Stokes Brothers' greengrocers in Tontine Street, where they had earlier received a delivery of potatoes. At 6.22pm, as the Gothas roared overhead, a bomb exploded outside the shop. The blast ripped through the people, mostly women and children, and smashed the shop. When the dust and smoke settled, 44 shattered bodies lay among the rubble, killed instantly, and another 17 soon succumbed to their injuries. No single

The plaque in Tontine Street, Folkestone, commemorates the victims of the first Gotha raid on Britain. The explosion in this street claimed the most civilian casualties inflicted by any single bomb throughout the war. The open space behind the plaque was occupied at the time by Stokes Brothers' greengrocer's shop. (Historic Military Press)

bomb in Britain throughout the war caused more civilian casualties.[93]

The Stokes family quickly rebuilt their business, reopening just 29 days later, and continued trading there until 1982. In 1985 a fire destroyed the building and the space where it stood remained vacant, a silent testimony to what had happened at that spot in May 1917.[94] Later the space became a beer garden for the Brewery Tap pub next door and more recently an arts charity acquired it, where in 2014 an arts project created a memorial garden. A plaque commemorating the bomb stands in Tontine Street, outside the garden. In 2017 plans for a temporary building to serve as an arts festival visitor centre received approval, but eventually this was located elsewhere. The fact that this is in an area of creative regeneration must, sadly, raise a question mark over the long-term future of the site.

Workman rebuilding Stokes Brothers' greengrocers in Tontine Street after the raid. It reopened for business just 29 days after the bomb destroyed it. (Courtesy of Les Haigh)

72

P.u.W Bombs

Germany's new aeroplane bomb

Work carried out in 1915 at Germany's *Prüfanstalt und Werft (P.u.W.) der Fliegertruppe* (Test Establishment and Works of the Aviation Troops) looked into improving the accuracy of their aerial bombs by introducing a new aerodynamic design. With the design receiving a positive report from the *Aerodynamischen Versuchsanstalt* (Aerodynamics Research Institute) at Göttingen, engineers at the optical works of C. P. Goerz, designed

A selection of P.u.W. bombs on display at the Royal Museum of the Armed Forces and Military History in Brussels.

an impact fuse and a delay mechanism for the P.u.W. bomb. Tests in November 1915 showed an explosive composition of TNT and hexanitrodiphenylamine proved to be the most effective. Other tests noted optimal stabilisation at 300 revolutions per minute on descent. This was made possible by fixing angled fins to the bomb, the smaller versions having three and the larger type's four fins. These rotations also produced the centrifugal force required to activate the fuse. The body of the bomb was formed of high-grade steel rather than the cast iron of earlier types, giving it greater penetrating power.[95] In Britain the shape of these new streamlined bombs led to them being referred to as 'aerial torpedoes'. They were in effect the prototype of the modern aircraft bomb.

There were six versions of the P.u.W. bomb, five high-explosive and one incendiary. All were carried in bomb racks. The 12kg, 50kg and incendiary bombs became available in 1916, the first 100kg and 300kg types in August 1917 followed by the 1,000kg bomb at the beginning of 1918. This last bomb was the heaviest to be dropped from the air during the war by any nation. Two were dropped on London by a modified 'Giant' bomber.

Weight	Length	Max. diameter
10kg (incendiary)	810mm	125mm
12kg	750mm	90mm
50kg	1,700mm	180mm
100kg	1,900mm	250mm
300kg	2,800mm	360mm
1,000kg	3,900mm	550mm[96]

The full range of P.u.W. high-explosive bombs: from left to right, 50kg, 100kg, 300kg, 1,000kg; the soldier is holding a 12.5kg bomb.

The bomb loads carried by the Gothas varied, with about 300kg loaded during daylight raids and up to 400kg at night. The combination of bomb weights could also vary. The P.u.W. incendiary bombs, however, proved a major disappointment for the Germans, as the historian Major Hilmer von Bülow explained:

'A great deal of time and effort had gone into the design of these incendiary bombs, on whose effect on the densely settled London area such high hopes were based. The bomb was a complete failure … The sound idea of creating panic and disorder with numerous fires came to nothing owing to the inadequacy of the materials employed.'[97]

The bombs shown on the previous page are in the collection of the Royal Museum of the Armed Forces and Military History in Brussels.

Relic of an Essex raid

On 5 June, while *Kagohl 3* awaited the weather to provide a clear opportunity to attack London, the squadron made a raid on secondary targets. Crossing the Essex coast between the rivers Blackwater and Crouch at about 6.15pm, the 21 Gothas headed towards Shoeburyness, where the artillery had training facilities and testing grounds. Having dropped bombs with little effect as they passed over Great Wakering and North Shoebury, two guns at the Anti-Aircraft School of Instruction and one on the Experimental Ranges opened fire as the Gothas passed over Shoeburyness. They caused the Gotha formation to scatter as it headed south over the Thames Estuary towards the naval docks at Sheerness.

At Shoeburyness over 20 bombs had fallen on the town and military facilities, with four high-explosive bombs landing close to barracks. Two of these, both 50kg high-explosive bombs, exploded on a grassy area in the Artillery Gun Park. The explosions killed one soldier and mortally wounded another, who died the following day. One severely injured horse had to be put down and another sustained injury but recovered.[98]

Members of the Anti-Aircraft School of Instruction recovered the nose section of one of these P.u.W. bombs. They mounted this fragment on a plinth and presented it to the officers of the Royal Artillery. It bears a plaque that states: 'Nose of bomb dropped by a German aeroplane on Shoeburyness during the air raid on June 5th 1917, in the course of which an enemy machine was shot down by anti-aircraft fire.' One Gotha, fired at by guns from Shoeburyness and Barton's Point, on the other side of the Thames Estuary, was shot down with the credit given to Barton's Point gun.

In 1920 the Royal Horse and Field Artillery branch of the School of Gunnery left Shoeburyness and moved to Larkhill in Wiltshire. This air raid relic moved with them and now resides in the Royal Artillery Officers' Mess and Quarters.

The nose section of the P.u.W. bomb dropped at Shoeburyness in Essex during the Gotha raid of 5 June 1917. (Historic Military Press)

73

Sopwith Pup N5182

A Home Defence aircraft that survived the war

The Sopwith Aviation Company introduced the Admiralty Type 9901 in 1916. This single-seater fighter, although officially named the Sopwith Scout, earned the popular nickname 'Pup' as it looked similar to the Sopwith 1½ Strutter but was smaller. The Pup was a light and manoeuvrable fighter with a good rate of climb and had an immediate impact when introduced on the Western Front with the RNAS in the autumn of 1916.

Sopwith Pup N5182 joined C Squadron, No. 1 Wing, RNAS, in September 1916 and her pilot, a Canadian, Flight Lieutenant E. R. Grange, shot down a German seaplane off the coast of Ostend on 25 September. In October 1916, N5182 transferred to No. 8 (Naval) Squadron, where her Australian pilot, Flight sub-Lieutenant

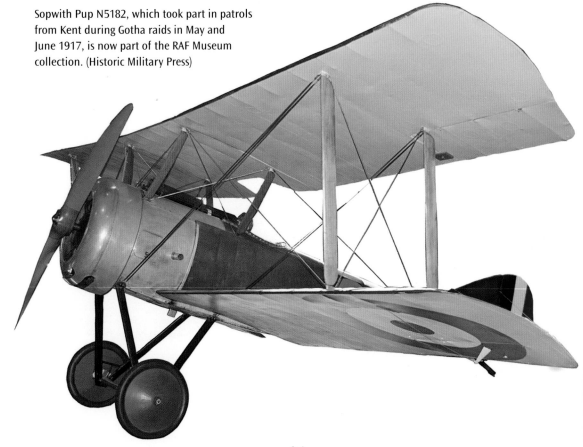

Sopwith Pup N5182, which took part in patrols from Kent during Gotha raids in May and June 1917, is now part of the RAF Museum collection. (Historic Military Press)

R. A. Little, brought down two enemy aircraft. On 3 February 1917, N5182 transferred to No. 3 (Naval) Squadron but, considered 'no longer useful', returned to the depot at Dunkirk a few days later. By April, with the Pup now outclassed by new German fighters, N5182 returned to England, allocated to Home Defence.[99]

On 25 May 1917, when the Gothas of *Kagohl 3* launched their first attempt on London, N5182 was stationed at RNAS Walmer. Flight sub-Lieutenant W. H. Chisam took off at 5.30pm in Sopwith Pup 9947, but returned 50 minutes later and then went up at 6.30pm in a Bristol Scout. Encountering more problems, he returned to Walmer, then took off again at 6.53pm in Pup N5182.[100] But by then the Gothas were already on their way home. When *Kagohl 3* returned on 5 June, N5182 took off from RNAS Dover at 6.20pm, patrolling for 85 minutes without finding the raiders.[101] Seemingly a reserve aircraft, N5182 saw no more action, switching to a training role at Manston later in 1917, before being withdrawn from service in February 1918.

At some point N5182 returned to France and in the late 1950s the remains – including fuselage, wings, 80hp Le Rhone engine and propeller – were discovered stored in an old airship shed holding the reserve collection of the *Musée de l'Air*. After a full restoration, taking 13 years to complete, Sopwith Pup N5182, received an Airworthiness Certificate in 1974 and took part in a number of air shows over the next two years, eventually becoming a part of the Royal Air Force Museum collection in 1998. The museum believes N5182 features 60–70 per cent original, or 'at least contemporary', components; she is currently on display at the Cosford site of the RAF Museum.

William Hargrove 'Harry' Chisam, RNAS. Chisam left England to start a new life in Canada in 1912. Three years later he went to America to learn to fly at Orville Wright's flying school at Dayton, Ohio, and returned to England in 1916 to enrol in the RNAS. He went on to shoot down 7 German aircraft on the Western Front earning him Ace status. In May 1917, while based at RNAS Walmer, Chisam flew Sopwith Pup N5182 when Gotha bombers made their first, aborted, attempt on London. (Courtesy of Margaret Chisam Partington)

74

Plaques to the Memory of PC Alfred Smith

A London policeman who gave his life so others may live

Alfred Smith served as a London policeman in 'G' Division, stationed at Shepherdess Walk, off City Road. He was aged 37, lived with his wife May and their three-year-old son, also called Alfred, at 22 Gerrard Street, Islington. During the night of 12/13 June 1917, Smith had suffered much from pains in his legs and had been unable to sleep. His wife urged him not to go to work in the morning as she thought he was not fit to do so, but he went on duty as normal at 8.30am on Wednesday, 13 June, 'as he thought it was his duty to go'. As he did so the Gothas of *Kagohl 3* were preparing to attack London.

As the morning approached midday, PC Smith was on point duty in Central Street, Islington, just north of its junction with Old Street. At the same time a formation of 14 Gothas approached London from the east. Bombs began to fall around 11.40am. Rhoda Pipe, one of 150 female workers employed at Debenham & Co based at Nos. 49–50 Central Street, was working in the basement when she heard a bang but initially thought someone upstairs had knocked over a stool. When she heard another, however, she shouted 'Bombs!'. Everyone rushed upstairs to

The ceramic plaque on the Memorial to Heroic Self Sacrifice located in 'Postman's Park' in London, installed in recognition of PC Smith's selfless actions during the first daylight Gotha raid on the capital.

ABOVE: The new plaque erected in Central Street by Islington Council on the centenary of PC Smith's actions.

LEFT: Police Constable Alfred Smith of G Division, Metropolitan Police. Despite a sleepless night, he went to work as normal on 13 June as he felt 'it was his duty to go'.

get out into the street, which Rhoda felt 'was the natural thing to do'.

Outside, in Central Street, PC Smith also heard the bombs. When he saw the door of Debenham's open and staff begin to emerge, he dashed forward. Rhoda described PC Smith putting his arm up to hold them back, and as he did so a bomb exploded in the street. The force of the blast struck PC Smith. All those crowded in the doorway escaped injury but Alfred Smith lay dead at their feet.[102] Two bombs fell in Central Street, killing 13 people,

but the death toll would have increased shockingly but for PC Smith's selfless act.

In recognition of his actions, on 13 June 1919, the second anniversary of his death, a commemorative ceramic plaque was installed on the Memorial to Heroic Self Sacrifice located in 'Postman's Park' in the City of London. Later, in 2017, on the centenary of his death, Islington Council erected a 'People's Plaque' on the building that now occupies Nos. 39–45 Central Street, where one of the two bombs exploded.

75

Sidney Elkin's Collar

A narrow escape from death

The first London daylight Gotha raid, on 13 June 1917, struck the capital in the late morning of a normal working Wednesday. Of the 118 bombs dropped on London, just seven fell south of the Thames, between Southwark and Bermondsey. At the premises of tea wholesalers British & Benington's Ltd, located at the corner of Southwark Road and Sumner Street, the sound of exploding bombs resulted in a variety of reactions. Many of the staff remained where they were, others headed to the company strong room, while some gathered near a lift shaft in the basement. But 19-year-old clerk Sidney Elkins, contrary to general advice, went out into the street, determined to witness the raid. Sidney stood in Sumner Street, looking north towards the sound of the bombs. At about 11.50am, a 50kg high-explosive bomb struck British & Benington's, just yards from where Sidney was standing.

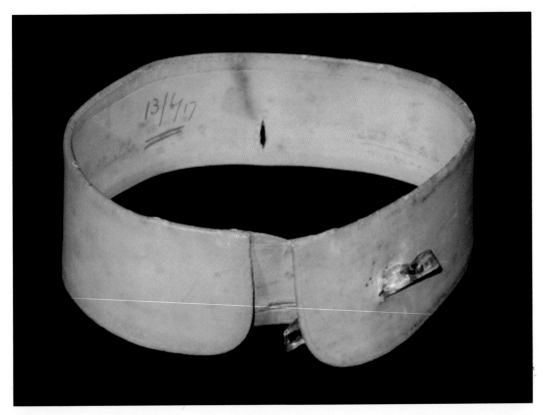

The collar Sidney Elkins wore to work on 13 June 1917 and which may have saved his life. The collar and shard of glass have remained a treasured family possession down the years. (Courtesy of Europeana 1914–1918)

Sidney Elkins and four of his brothers in a photograph believed to have been taken after the war. Sidney Elkins is in the back row on the right. (Courtesy of Europeana 1914–1918)

The bomb struck the rear of the premises, obliterating a two-storey store and inflicting serious damage on the five-storey main part of the building. A chaos of rubble, dust and smoke filled the shattered building, trapping many of those inside. Rescuers were quick to arrive. One 'badly mutilated' woman died instantly, while 26 people sustained shocking injuries, from which two girls later died.[103]

Sidney Elkins was in Sumner Street when the bomb exploded on his place of work.[104] The blast sent shards of plate glass scything through the air and smashed windows in buildings all along Sumner Street and others in Holland Street. Small pieces of flying glass inflicted minor cuts to Sidney's head and face but a larger, potentially lethal piece, measuring two and a half inches in length, arrowed towards his neck. Sidney was wearing a stiff detachable collar to his shirt, as he always did at work. The shard of glass struck his collar, which took the full impact and prevented it from penetrating his neck. It may have saved his life. Well aware of how lucky he had been, Sidney kept that collar, complete with glass shard, which has passed down through the family in the intervening years as a sobering reminder of how close Sidney Elkins came to death on the streets of London. He later joined the army and survived the war.

76

Upper North Street School Memorials
Plaistow and Poplar, London
Marking the tragedy of London's first Gotha raid

Of all the bombs dropped on London on 13 June 1917 in the first daylight Gotha raid, one above all others left an indelible mark on the city. After the raiders had released most of their bombs over central London, those still carrying them as they headed away from the capital dropped them over east London. One hurtled down on Poplar, towards a school in Upper North Street.

The bomb smashed through the roof of the school, crashing through a girls' classroom on the top floor and then on through a boys' classroom on the next floor, killing two children in its path. From there it penetrated down to the ground

The marker over the mass grave of 15 of the 18 children killed in the tragedy at Upper North Street School. The grave is in the East London Cemetery, Plaistow.

A close-up of the grave marker showing the names and ages of the 15 children buried in the mass grave.

floor, where it finally exploded in a room divided into two containing 64 infants and their teachers. The blast of the bomb decimated the classroom, killing 16 children all aged five or six and injuring many more.

This tragic incident of that first Gotha raid shocked the East End. The Mayor of Poplar announced that all the children would be interred in one grave 'so they should not be separated even in death'. He then added that, 'When the time comes a memorial expressing our sympathy will be placed above them.'[105]

In fact, only 15 of the 18 children were buried in a mass grave in the East London Cemetery, Plaistow, on 20 June. The three other children were buried privately, two in St Patrick's Roman Catholic Cemetery, Leytonstone, and one in

Abney Park Cemetery, Stoke Newington. A public fund to raise money for a grave marker surpassed expectations and easily raised the amount needed; the additional money paid for the erection of a memorial to the children in Poplar Recreation Ground on East India Dock Road and supported three children's hospital beds.

The grave marker, resembling an outcrop of stone, bears a carved scroll on which is an inscription: 'This memorial is erected to the memory of the children interred here who lost their lives at North St School Poplar during the hostile air raid on June 13th 1917.' The scroll also lists the names of the 15 children buried in the grave.

The memorial in Poplar, surmounted by an angel in mourning, was unveiled on 23 June 1919 and lists the names of all 18 children killed at the school.

LEFT: The memorial to those killed by the bomb that struck the Upper North Street School, Poplar, on 13 June 1917. The memorial, erected in the Poplar Recreation Ground, was paid for using excess money raised for the grave marker.

BELOW LEFT and RIGHT: Panels on the memorial listing the names and ages of the 18 victims of the Upper Street North School tragedy.

77

Souvenir Napkin – 13 June 1917

The funeral procession that halted London's East End

The funeral of the children killed at the Upper North Street School, Poplar, by a bomb dropped from a German Gotha on 13 June 1917 brought that part of London to a standstill. As *The Times* put it:

'A hard life has not hardened the dwellers in dockland. Behind the dingy and often squalid exterior of the East End there lies a rich fount of human emotion. Sometimes it wells up and makes one marvel at the great heart of the toilers in these mean and crowded streets … The pulsing industrial and commercial life of the district was stilled for a while, and in its place there appeared a throbbing community of sorrow.'[106]

Those 'mean streets' were crowded with thousands of respectful East Enders on 20 June 1917 for the children's funeral procession. The service, which took place at All Saints' Church, Poplar, was conducted by the Bishop of London,

A souvenir napkin produced by printers S. Burgess 'in loving memory' of the victims of the 13 June 1917 Gotha raid on London, the first of the two daytime raids on the capital.

The funeral procession of the child victims of the Poplar school bomb bringing the East End of London to a halt. The inset photograph shows how great the impact could be on those listed among the injured.

the Bishop of Stepney and the rector of Poplar, and attended by the families of the children, staff and children from the Upper North Street School, as well as Government officials and representatives of trade unions and local businesses. In the church 16 coffins stood on trestles, covered in wreaths, of which over 500 had been received from individuals, schools, hospitals, businesses, official bodies and market traders. The coffins contained the bodies of the 15 children destined to lie in the mass grave and one held 'fragments of bodies' that remained unidentifiable. After the service at the church, the coffins were placed in eight horse-drawn hearses, each covered with wreaths, and the cortege led

the way to the East London Cemetery about two and a half miles away, followed by a 'train of carriages'. They passed through silent crowds lining the streets three or four deep.

As a memento of this solemn occasion, the printers S. Burgess produced souvenir paper napkins (see Object 23), of which there were at least two versions. The one shown here commemorates the raid in general, while one in the collection of the Imperial War Museum has the same black-edged wording but with the addition of the names of the children killed at the school and a different floral border. Cheap to produce and cheap to buy, these souvenirs proved highly popular.

78

Glove from the Crew of L 48
Theberton, Suffolk
Poignant items from the crew's last mission

Just three days after the first Gotha attack on London, with the capital still coming to terms with this new development in the air war, the Naval Airship Division launched a Zeppelin raid targeting the city. Bad weather conditions and mechanical failures, however, meant that only two reached England. One of these, L 48, commanded by Franz Georg Eichler, also had Korvettenkapitän Viktor Schütze on board. Schütze's appointment as commander of the Naval Airship Division followed Peter Strasser's promotion to *Führer der Luftschiffe* (Leader of Airships) in November 1916.

L 48 spent well over two hours off the Suffolk coast, struggling with engine problems and a frozen compass, before coming inland at about 2am on 17 June. Too late to attack London,

A very personal relic from L 48; a leather glove worn by one of the crew on his last raid over England. (Courtesy of the Long Shop Museum, Leiston)

Eichler selected Harwich as a secondary target. However, at 2.45am, when the Harwich guns opened fire, L 48 turned away to the north, heading over Suffolk and dropping bombs on a number of villages. Flying at 14,000 feet, with his engines continuing to cause problems, Eichler received a radio message advising him of a helpful tail wind at 11,000 feet.

Alerted to news of a Zeppelin approaching the Suffolk coast, aircraft took off from the RFC's Orfordness Experimental Station and from No. 37 Squadron's airfield at Goldhanger. Now illuminated against the lightening summer sky, these aircraft soon found the struggling L 48 and attacked. In moments explosive and incendiary bullets turned her menacing black-painted bulk into a 'mass of flame'. She hurtled down towards the ground to smash into a field at Holly Tree Farm in Theberton.

Incredibly, three of the crew survived the fall: Leutnant-zur-See Otto Mieth and two machinists, Wilhelm Uecker and Heinrich Ellerkamm. The other 16 men on board, including Kapitänleutnant Franz Georg Eichler and Viktor Schütze, all died.

Once the flames took hold, Otto Mieth realised the end was near and decided a quick death was preferable to burning alive. He was about to jump when the command gondola lurched backwards, burying Mieth under a heap of struggling comrades as the flames spread towards them. 'It grew fearfully hot. I felt the flames against my face … I wrapped my arms about my head to protect it from the scorching flames, hoping the end would come quickly. That was the last I remember.'[107]

The shock of the crash brought Mieth briefly back to consciousness. 'I remember a thrill of horror as I opened my eyes and saw myself surrounded by a sea of flames and red-hot metal beams and braces that seemed to crush me. Then I lost consciousness a second time.'

Rescuers dragged Mieth from the burning wreckage; both his legs were broken and he had suffered serious burns, but he survived. Heinrich Ellerkamm had climbed high up inside the

ABOVE LEFT and RIGHT: The two German uniform buttons recovered from the crash site of Zeppelin L 48 during metal detector surveys in 2006 as part of an archaeological exploration of the site filmed for the BBC's *Timewatch* series. (Courtesy of Julian Evan-Hart)

framework as L 48 plummeted and this saved him. Rescuers found him wandering, bewildered near the wreckage. Willing hands pulled Wilhelm Uecker's badly burnt body from the starboard engine gondola but after examination he was found to have serious internal injuries from which he never recovered; he eventually died on 11 November 1918 – Armistice Day.

Those scouring the crash site recovered a number of personal items belonging to the crew. One such item was a leather glove now in the collection of the Long Shop Museum in Leiston, Suffolk. Others only appeared in 2006 when an archaeological examination took place at the crash site.[108] Although little significant material emerged, two personal items did, revealed by metal detectors; buttons from uniforms of the crew of L 48. They lay undisturbed in the soil for 89 years but now present a tangible link to the last desperate moments of another of Germany's doomed Zeppelin raiders.

Risen from the Wreckage

As was standard practice, engineers of the Admiralty's Constructional Department arrived to inspect the wreckage of L 48, measuring all components and recording all they found. This information would add to that gleaned from the skeleton of L 33 back in September 1916 and be used in Britain's own post-war rigid airship programme. The information gathered from L 48 was utilised in Britain's R.36 airship launched in 1921. Once this recording had finished, personnel from the Admiralty and RNAS cut up the wreckage over the next few weeks and transported it by road to Leiston railway station, its ultimate destination unknown. Local people were quick to acquire any pieces that literally 'fell off the back of a lorry' and turn them into souvenirs. A number of these are on display in the Long Shop Museum, Leiston. One large piece of L 48's framework on display in a glass case at St Peter's Church, Theberton, however, is likely to have been donated to the village by the authorities.

STRAFED ZEPP. L48, June 17, 1917.   No 8   J. S. Waddell, Photo, Leiston

ABOVE LEFT: A large section of duralumin girder from Zeppelin L 48 donated to St Peter's Church, Theberton.

ABOVE RIGHT: A postcard showing the great tangle of bent and twisted duralumin girders of L 48 lying in a field on Holly Tree Farm.

79

St Peter's Church Cemetery
Theberton, Suffolk

The burial of the crew of Zeppelin L 48

The inquest and burial of the crew of Zeppelin L 48 took place on 20 June 1917. Two bodies still lay undetected under the wreckage so the inquest presided over the bodies of 14 of the 16 dead crew. It took place at Holly Tree Farm, where the bodies lay in a barn.

The military recovered 13 bodies on the day of the crash, with one more discovered the following day. Five of these, including the commander of L 48, Kapitänleutnant Franz Georg Eichler, had jumped to their deaths. An army medical officer described how 'all of them had bones broken and heads smashed'. Six bodies found near the command gondola 'were badly burnt and there was no chance of identifying them in any way'. A body still sitting in the port engine gondola 'was not burned', a police officer explained, he had 'fallen forward and knocked his face in'. The final, badly burnt body discovered on the first day was lying in wreckage near the starboard engine gondola. The following day, a body found under wreckage near the aft engine had all its clothes burnt off.[109]

Later the same day, four horse-drawn gun carriages and three army wagons transported the bodies the half a mile to St Peter's Church, Theberton, where the funeral took place in the

The replacement sign denoting the original burial site of the crew of Zeppelin L 48 before their transfer to the German cemetery at Cannock Chase in the 1960s.

cemetery across the road from the churchyard. A wreath placed on Eichler's coffin (documents found on his body identified Eichler) bore the words, 'To a very brave enemy from RFC officers'. A mass grave measuring 24 feet long, nine feet eight inches wide and six feet deep held all 14 coffins. A large crowd, both military and civilian, gathered to watch respectfully as the crew of L 48 were laid to rest. Two days later the final two 'badly mutilated and partly burnt' bodies were recovered from the wreckage and buried on 23 June with their comrades. The RFC then marked the plot with a signboard bearing a fitting verse from the New Testament (Romans 14:4): 'Who art thou that judgest another man's servant? To his own master he standeth or falleth.' When that fell into disrepair a replacement sign took its place, bearing a shortened version of the verse.

The shortened version of the original text on the replacement sign.

The original sign in front of the Zeppelin crew's graves in the small cemetery at Church Road, Theberton, opposite the church hall. (The David Marks Collection)

An aerial view of the crash site showing military cordons keeping visitors back from the wreckage while investigations are under way.

A bullet fired at L 48

During a metal detector survey of the crash site in 2006, detectorists unearthed a British bullet. Surprisingly, it was not one of the explosive or incendiary bullets, but a standard .303 round, and damage to the nose suggests it had hit something hard. These bullets were not regularly used during Zeppelin patrols. However, a D.H.2 from the Orfordness Experimental Station, piloted by Captain R. H. M. S. Saundby, went up at 2.55am, although it was not set up for night flying. In his subsequent report, the commander at Orfordness, Major P. C. Cooper, reported that Saundby had only 47-round single drums of ammunition on board, not the double 97-round drum, and fired one of Buckingham incendiary bullets, one of SPG 'Sparklet' tracers and one of Mark VII S.A. Ball, the standard .303 bullet. It seems likely, therefore, that the bullet found at the crash site was one fired by Captain Saundby. While it would not have ignited L 48's hydrogen, the 'nick' to the nose of the bullet certainly appears to suggest it was on target.

The bullet – Mark VII S.A. Ball – recovered from the crash site by metal detectorists during the archaeological survey carried out in 2006. (Courtesy of Julian Evan-Hart)

80

Church of St Edmund the King & Martyr
Lombard Street, City of London

A bomb preserved on the spot where it landed

On the morning of Saturday, 7 July 1917, the second daylight Gotha raid struck London. As in the previous daytime raid, the majority of bombs fell roughly in a one-mile radius of Liverpool Street Station. About 16 bombs fell between Moorgate and Fenchurch Street; within this area stood the Bank of England, one of Germany's prime targets. With considerable good fortune the bombs missed that target but many other buildings nearby suffered damage. A policeman, Thomas White, was on duty outside Mansion House as the Gothas approached. 'I stood on the steps and watched them. They were flying quite low, swooping down and up again like crows in flight. They passed over George Yard, Lombard Street and dropped a very heavy bomb which failed to explode.'[110]

In fact, there is a little confusion about whether one or two bombs fell in Lombard Street. The London Fire Brigade report states that two fell on the church of St Edmund the King & Martyr, where one failed to detonate. The police report, however, states a bomb exploded on the church

Fragments of the bomb that smashed through the roof of the Church of St Edmund the King & Martyr in Lombard Street, London. These fragments are in a glass case that is now an integral part of the altar.

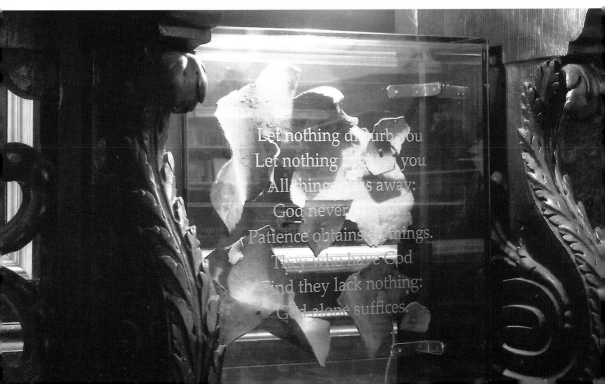

and another, which failed to detonate, struck an office building next door at No. 60. Then, to confuse matters further, a summary report compiled by the Intelligence Section, General Headquarters, Home Forces, in September 1917 lists only an unexploded bomb on the church. Having looked through the records, I am inclined to accept the police report in this instance. Inside the church, in a glass case fixed under the altar, are the broken and twisted fragments of the bomb that struck the church. On the glass front is the prayer of St Teresa of Avila, which starts with the words, 'Let nothing disturb you, let nothing frighten you'. It certainly appears to have exploded, although perhaps it did not explode

with full force. The bomb smashed through the roof, breaking the main supporting beam and causing damage inside the church. Although both the police and fire brigade describe this damage as slight, the roof required a complete replacement and the church did not reopen its doors until October 1919.

There remains another interesting reminder of this incident in the church. The architects who designed the new roof built a square window into it to mark where the bomb had smashed down into the church.

Although still consecrated, the church no longer holds regular services and is home to the London Centre for Spiritual Direction.

During repairs to the church's roof, damaged by the bomb dropped from a Gotha, a square window was created marking the point where the bomb smashed through. (Historic Military Press)

81

16ᵗʰ Century Chest, Ironmongers' Hall
Fenchurch Street, City of London
A silent witness to the force of a Gotha bomb

After dropping the bomb in Lombard Street that smashed the roof of the Church of St Edmund the King & Martyr, the Gothas continued on their course over the City of London. A Mr Shardlow saw them approaching Fenchurch Street:

'A pal and I were standing in Mark Lane … when suddenly we heard the drone of aeroplane engines. There, coming towards us, was a whole flight, flying very low. We watched fascinated. And then suddenly they dropped a bomb clean on Ironmongers' Hall.'[111]

The headquarters of the Worshipful Company of Ironmongers, one of the City of London's 12 Great Livery Companies, had been in Fenchurch Street since the first Hall was established there in 1457. Although replaced twice, the Hall had survived on this spot, on the north side of Fenchurch Street by the junction with Billiter Street, for 460 years. Now a German bomb hurtled down towards it.

There were eight or nine people in the building at the time, but when they first heard the sound of exploding bombs they sought shelter in the basement. The bomb exploded in the central courtyard of the Hall. It gouged a great crater in the paving, hurling lumps of stone for up to 100 yards. Within the confines of the Hall the blast blew out window frames, wrenched doors off their hinges and caused irreparable damage to some of the fine decorative features inside.

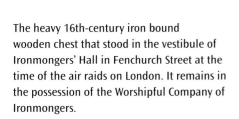

The heavy 16th-century iron bound wooden chest that stood in the vestibule of Ironmongers' Hall in Fenchurch Street at the time of the air raids on London. It remains in the possession of the Worshipful Company of Ironmongers.

Those who had made their way to the basement were safe but the explosion jammed the door shut. They had to endure a testing time trapped in the pitch black of the basement before they were able to break free and emerge from their ordeal.[112]

In the vestibule of the Hall stood a stout 16th-century iron-bound wooden chest. The force of the blast sent it skidding eight feet across the floor. Bomb fragments appear to have struck

the rear of the chest, causing a splintering effect inside, while one pierced the back near the top of the chest. It seared its way across the underside of the lid to emerge at the front, damaging one of the iron hasps. After the war, the Worshipful Company of Ironmongers built a new Hall in Shaftesbury Place, Aldersgate Street. The iron chest, unrepaired from its encounter with the bomb on 7 July 1917, found a new home in the entrance hall.

Deep gouges and holes in the chest's timber show where bomb fragments stuck it, sending it skidding eight feet across the floor.

Bomb damage in the central courtyard of Ironmongers' Hall on Fenchurch Street. Great lumps of stone from the bomb crater were flung over buildings for up to 100 yards.

82

Iron Cross, 1ˢᵗ Class

Among the 21 aircraft of *Kagohl 3* that attacked London in the second daylight raid on 7 July 1917, was Gotha G.IV 406/16, commanded by Leutnant Adolf Genth, with pilot Leutnant G. Radke and rear gunner, Vizefeldwebel Kurt Gaede. They had already taken part in the raids on Folkestone on 25 May and London on 13 June. Now they headed for London again.

Having attended a military school and served as a cadet, when war broke out in 1914, Adolf Genth held the rank of leutnant in *4. Magdeburger Infanterie Regiment Nr.67.* Serving on the Western Front, he received

Adolf Genth's medals: Iron Cross 1st Class, Knight's Cross and Honour Medal. Genth received the Iron Cross 1st Class for his participation in the daylight Gotha raids on London in the summer of 1917. (Courtesy of Thomas Genth)

the Iron Cross 2nd Class in November 1914, but three wounds in two years left him with a weakened left arm, leading Genth to transfer to the *Fliegertruppe* in July 1916. After training as an observer, he joined *Halbgeschwader 1* on 10 October 1916. Here he met pilot Leutnant G. Radke, with whom he served for the rest of the war. In November 1916 a new bomber unit was authorised – *Kampfgeschwader 3 der OHL (Kagohl 3)* – formed on a nucleus of personnel from *Halbgeschwader 1*, including Genth.[113]

Returning from London on 7 July, over 100 Home Defence aircraft took off to try to intercept the Gothas of *Kagohl 3*. One attacked Genth's Gotha. With Genth manning the front machine gun, and Gaede the rear one, the crew had a lively engagement with an aircraft they described as an 'English single-seater'. The German crew reported the British aircraft had gone down somewhere 'near London'.

After a long delay their victory received official confirmation.

For his participation in the daylight raids on London, Genth received the Iron Cross 1st Class. He continued to fly with *Kagohl 3* and a year later, on 7 June 1918, became the squadron's adjutant. In all, Genth flew 11 missions over England. From June 1918 Genth and Radke flew two-seater night fighters on the Western Front, shooting down a British Handley Page 0/400 bomber on the night of 30 June 1918. That same day Genth's award of the Knight's Cross with Swords of the Royal House Order of Hohenzollern was authorised. The photo on the previous page shows Adolf Genth's Iron Cross 1st Class, Knight's Cross and Honour Medal, all of which remain with his family.

Adolf Genth flew again in the Second World War but died of his wounds after a Hurricane attacked his Dornier Do 17Z over Dover on 29 July 1940.

Adolf Genth's *Beobachterabzeichen* or Observer's Badge, awarded in January 1917. Observers only received their badges after completing a requisite number of hours of operational flying. (Courtesy of Thomas Genth)

Adolf Genth's Gotha of *Kagohl 3* en route to London on 7 July 1917 in the second London daylight raid. As commander, Genth occupies the nacelle in the nose of the aircraft, and was responsible for navigation, bomb aiming and operating the forward machine gun. The caption under the photo was written by Adolf Genth. (Courtesy of Thomas Genth)

A photograph of Adolf Genth taken during the Second World War. He proudly wears his Iron Cross and Observer's Badge awarded in the First World War. (Courtesy of Thomas Genth)

2ⁿᵈ Lt Wilfred Salmon's 'Wings'
The first pilot killed in combat defending London

On 7 July the RFC and RNAS flew 108 sorties to oppose the second daylight raid launched against London by *Kagohl 3*. One of those sorties proved to be the first and last flown by 2nd Lieutenant Wilfred Graham Salmon.

'Wiff' Salmon, born to English parents in Australia in 1894, joined the Australian Imperial Force in July 1915 as an artillery driver. While serving on the Somme in November 1916 he secured a transfer to the Royal Flying Corps for pilot training. He did well and arrived at No. 63 (Training) Squadron based at Joyce Green, near Dartford, on the outskirts of London in June 1917 to complete his training. He received a probationary commission as 2nd lieutenant in the Royal Flying Corps on 20 June 1917.

On the morning of 7 July, warning of an approaching Gotha formation was issued at 9.24am and pilots all over the south-east took to their aircraft; just 17 days after receiving his commission, Salmon, flying a Sopwith Pup single-seater fighter, was one of them.

Salmon had been in the air for about an hour when he saw the Gothas returning from London and made his attack. He fired 55 rounds from his machine gun but he was also on the end of a deadly return fire. A bullet passed right through his petrol tank, which immediately began to drain, another cut one of his control wires and one struck him, slashing across his forehead.

Although seeing the pilot in difficulty, his acting squadron commander felt he would make it back to Joyce Green. Anticipating a landing, he looked away for a moment but when he turned back, Salmon's Sopwith Pup had crashed. Pulled from the wreckage, Salmon was dead, his skull 'fractured from ear to ear'.[114] Although the two-man crew of

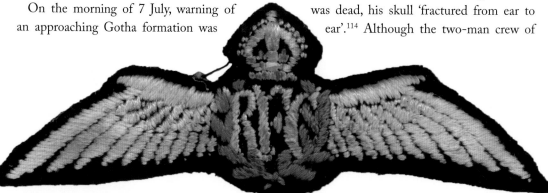

Wilfred Salmon's pilot's wings, worn on his tunic the day he was killed while defending London. (Courtesy of Ballarat Clarendon College, Australia)

another RFC aircraft were killed that day, it appears Salmon's death was earlier, earning him the unwelcome distinction of becoming the first pilot killed in combat defending London, and only the second person since the Dutch sailed up the River Medway in 1667.* Two Gotha crews claimed shooting down a single-seater fighter but Germany credited the 'kill' to Gotha G.IV 406/16, commanded by Leutnant Adolf Genth (see Object 82).

After a funeral service at Holy Trinity Church, Wilfred Salmon's Union Flag draped coffin was drawn on a gun-carriage through the silent, respectful crowds that lined the streets of Dartford to Watling Street cemetery, where his body was laid to rest.

*During the first Gotha raid on London on 13 June 1917, Captain Cecil Horace Case Keevil, an observer flying in a Bristol Fighter of No. 35 (Training) Squadron, became the first man killed in combat while defending London for 250 years.

A picture of 2nd Lieutenant Wilfred Graham Salmon, RFC, taken shortly before he went into action for the first – and last – time.

LEFT and BELOW: Wilfred Salmon's grave in Dartford's Watling Road cemetery. Injured while attacking a Gotha returning from a daylight raid on London, he died in the wreckage of his crashed aircraft.

84

Matchbox Cover

A souvenir made from the wreckage of a Gotha

After the two daylight raids on London, weather conditions over Britain proved unfavourable for raiding the capital; instead *Kagohl 3* focused on coastal towns in south-east England. Raids took place on 22 July, 12 August and 22 August.

In the last of these, ten Gothas approached Margate on the Kent coast, but the defence organisation was on the alert with pilots in the air and AA guns ready for action. RNAS pilots attacked as the raiders neared Margate and one Gotha crashed down into the sea before it reached land. Moments later, as the formation crossed the coast, another found itself in trouble, this time from the guns. An officer of the Home Defence Intelligence Corps described how a shell burst under the wing and lifted the aircraft. He continued:

'The machine at once swung round to the West and a few seconds afterwards burst into flames and commenced to glide down at a very steep angle. When it arrived over about the centre of the Hengrove Golf Course, just East of the Hengrove gun, an engine fell out of the machine, followed almost immediately by the breaking off of a wing. The machine then swung round to the South and gliding at an angle of about 45° – 60° finally struck the ground in an oat field at a point about 300 yards East of

Vincent Farm. The occupier of the farm ran at once to the spot and made an attempt to rescue the occupants of the machine who were unconscious, but he thought might be alive. He was, however, driven off by the explosion of the

A matchbox cover made from metal salvaged from the wreckage of a Gotha brought down near Margate on 22 August 1917. (Historic Military Press)

machine gun ammunition. The wreckage burnt fiercely for about an hour.'[115]

From newspaper reports it appears that the engine fell near Westgate and the wing came down on the Hengrove Golf Course before the main body of the Gotha crashed in the farmer's field. The crew, Oberleutant Echart Fulda, Unteroffizier Heinrich Schildt and Vizefeldwebel Ernst Eichelkamp, died in the fire.

This Gotha was the first brought down on land and there are two known artist's impressions of her last moments, one showing the point when the wing broke free and another about a second before the main body hit the ground. Parts of the wreckage were sold to raise funds for war charities, but the size of a Gotha when compared to that of a Zeppelin means that Gotha relics are much harder to find today than those from the four Zeppelins that crashed on British soil. Matchbox covers, however, are known from both Gotha and Zeppelin wrecks.

An artist's image of the Gotha hit by AA fire over Margate. Sold as a postcard, the image shows the point when the Gotha's wing broke off, as reported by eyewitnesses.

A Stirring Episode in the Raid of 22nd Aug., 1917.

Another artist's impression of the last moments of the Gotha, minus a wing, as it is about to crash on farmland with the coast and the town of Margate in the background.

85

The Drill Hall
Chatham, Kent

The highest death toll of any single air raid incident during the First Blitz

With mounting losses sustained by *Kagohl 3* during the summer of 1917, a switch to night raids began in September 1917. After a brief period of training, the first of these took place on the night of 3/4 September when five volunteer crews set out to target the Royal Navy shore base at Chatham, Kent, known as HMS *Pembroke*.

The new naval barracks at Chatham, opened in 1903, included a vast drill hall about 250 yards long, which provided indoor space for training and exercise during bad weather, but it also served as overflow accommodation when all the barrack blocks were full. On the night of 3 September it served that purpose with about 700 men (some sources say 900) accommodated, sleeping in hammocks under the glass roof. No one appeared concerned by the sound of approaching aircraft as an aerial training exercise had taken place earlier; all the lights in the town remained illuminated. At 11.12pm two high-explosive bombs smashed through the glass roof of the drill hall before

Despite the passing of 100 years and extensive restoration work at the Chatham drill hall, the track of one of the two bombs, which struck the building with such devastating effect, remains preserved in the roof's supporting girders. (Historic Military Press)

exploding on the concrete floor among the sleeping or relaxing naval personnel, the blast gouging craters about three feet across.

The scene inside the hall was horrific. Great shards of jagged glass cut and slashed their way through the closely packed sailors lying in their hammocks. One of the rescuers described the scene that greeted them: 'It was a gruesome task. Everywhere we found bodies in a terribly mutilated condition. Some with arms and legs missing and some headless. The gathering up of dismembered limbs turned one sick.'[116] It took 17 hours before the rescue and recovery work ended. Another helper recalled spending the night, 'picking out bodies, and parts of bodies, from among glass and debris and placing them in bags, fetching out bodies in hammocks and laying

them on a tarpaulin on the parade ground ... It was one of the most terrible nights I have ever known'.[117]

About 90 men died instantly, with the death toll eventually rising to 130. On 6 September the first 98 bodies were buried at Woodlands Cemetery, Gillingham, later joined by those who died of their injuries. A large cross was erected in the cemetery in memory of those who lost their lives. The families of 25 of the victims chose private burials.

The Chatham Naval Barracks closed in 1984 but the restored Grade 2 listed drill hall reopened in 2006 as the Drill Hall Library of the Universities at Medway. Despite the extensive renovations, evidence of the raid is still visible in the roof's supporting girders.

The former Chatham drill hall, now serving as the Drill Hall Library of the Universities at Medway. The layout remains the same as the original building. The bombs struck the building to the centre of the photograph, just to the right of the large gateway.

A small fragment of one of the bombs that struck the Chatham drill hall. A group of bomb fragments from the hall are in the collection of Chatham Historic Dockyard. (Historic Military Press)

A plaque by the entrance to the Drill Hall Library commemorating the great loss of life there in September 1917.

A pre-war postcard showing Naval ratings inside the vast drill hall.

The Chatham air raid memorial cross, unveiled at Gillingham's Woodlands Cemetery on 27 November 1918. It bears the inscription: 'To the glory of God and in sacred memory of all those who gave their lives for their country during the air raid by the enemy on the Royal Naval Barracks Chatham, 3rd Sept. 1917.'

86

Cleopatra's Needle
Victoria Embankment, London

Bearing the scars of London's first
night-time Gotha raid

The ancient Egyptian obelisk erected on the Victoria Embankment in London in 1878 originally stood in the Egyptian city of Heliopolis, erected there in about 1450 BC and later moved to Alexandria. In 1820 the obelisk was gifted to King George IV but only in 1877 was a plan to move it to London successful.

After the first night raid by *Kagohl 3* on Chatham the previous evening, on the night of 4/5 September 1917, the Gothas targeted London at night for the first time. Of 11 bombers that set out, five battled their way through to the capital.

One of the Gothas commenced its bombing run over Oxford Circus and headed south towards

The heavily impacted pedestal of the right-hand Sphinx guarding Cleopatra's Needle, blasted by the bomb that exploded on Victoria Embankment in London.

the River Thames, dropping three more bombs near the Strand. At the same time a single-decker tram had crossed Westminster Bridge and was heading along Victoria Embankment towards the Kingsway Tunnel. When the driver, Alfred Buckle, heard the sound of exploding bombs he accelerated, but just as he reached Cleopatra's Needle a 50kg bomb exploded on the pavement between the ancient monument and the tram. The powerful blast penetrated the pavement, where it smashed a gas main but also struck the tram with great force. A fragment of bomb or stone from the monument struck Buckle, 'his leg being practically blown off and broken in two places'. An eyewitness described how Buckle 'appeared to kneel down suddenly, still pulling at his controls', an action that earned him praise from his employers, who remarked on his 'strong sense of duty' although

severely injured. Bleeding profusely from his legs, rescuers took Buckle to hospital but he died before they got there. Two passengers on the tram also died: Amy Cuthbert, a waitress, and Richard McCaughin, a postal sorter, but the conductor, Joseph Carr staggered clear.[118]

The blast also sent bomb fragments smashing into the obelisk and one of the two bronze Sphinxes guarding the monument and its pedestal. The damage remains unrepaired in silent testimony to what happened there during London's first moonlight Gotha raid. A plaque added to the right-hand Sphinx pedestal incorrectly identifies the raid as 'the first raid on London by German aeroplanes'; it should perhaps be described as the first night-time aeroplane squadron raid, as a single German aircraft had made a night attack on the capital back in May 1917.

A close-up of damage inflicted to the paw of the Sphinx and the upper part of the pedestal.

Post-raid repairs under way to a damaged gas main running under Victoria Embankment in front of the damaged Sphinx. (Historic Military Press)

Gouges on the base of Cleopatra's Needle caused by the bomb just before midnight on 4 September 1917 during the first night-time Gotha raid on London.

87

Pigeon N.U.R.P./17/F.16331
'A Very Gallant Gentleman'
The vital work of the carrier pigeon

On 5 September 1917, following an engagement with Zeppelin L 44 over the North Sea, two British aircraft from RNAS Great Yarmouth came under fire from German naval vessels. Shell fragments damaged both aircraft, a D.H.4 and a Curtiss H.12 'Large America' flying boat (No. 8666). The D.H.4 crashed in the sea and the accompanying H.12, despite its own problems, landed to make a rescue. The four-man crew of the H.12 picked up the two men from the D.H.4, but the damaged and now overloaded flying boat began taking in water. Unable to take off, the commander of the H.12, Fight Commander Vincent Nicholl, ordered his pilot, Flight Lieutenant Robert Leckie, to start taxiing towards England, some 75 miles away. The men were all aware they lacked enough fuel for the journey and that they had only two gallons of drinking water and no food. With their telegraphy apparatus waterlogged, their only hope of rescue rested with four carrier pigeons. At 4pm Nicholl released two of the pigeons with messages indicating their circumstances and approximate position. Only one got through. Pigeon N.U.R.P./17/F.16331 battled its way to the Norfolk coast but died of exhaustion, its body only discovered three days later. By then the information was out of date, but help was at hand for the desperate airmen.

For three days and nights the H.12 floundered in a heavy sea. The six men on board, all suffering badly from seasickness, not only had to constantly bail water but they had to take turns to sit out on the port wing, constantly exposed to the icy sea, endeavouring to keep the damaged starboard wing out of the water. It was a nightmarish existence. Nicoll had released a third pigeon on the morning of 6 September but that too was lost. Later that day, at 3pm, he released the last bird, knowing their fate rested upon its wings. A little under 20 hours later, at 10.45am on 7 September, the pigeon reached land. From the note it carried a rescue boat from RNAS Great Yarmouth, HMS *Halcyon*, was able to locate the desperate crew, bringing them and the flying boat back to safety.[119]

Grateful to the pigeons for their part in the rescue, the airmen had the body of N.U.R.P./17/F.16331 preserved in a glass case, giving it a place of honour in the officers' mess at Great Yarmouth. Now in the collection of the RAF Museum in Hendon, the case bears a brass plaque with the words, 'A very gallant gentlemen', chosen by the men who were rescued due to the efforts of their pigeons.

'A very gallant gentleman'. So named by the officers at RNAS Great Yarmouth after the pigeon died of exhaustion while attempting to return with a message from the crews of two downed aircraft that had been engaged in a Zeppelin patrol over the North Sea. (Courtesy of the Trustees of the RAF Museum/Iain Duncan)

Curtiss H.12 'Large America' flying boat No. 8666, which, although damaged, landed in the North Sea to rescue the crew of a downed D.H.4 after an engagement with Zeppelin L 44, and was unable to take off again. (Courtesy of the Philip Jarrett Collection)

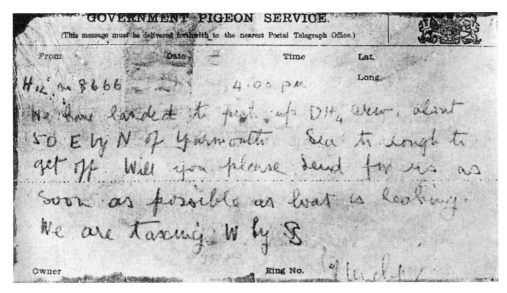

The message written by Flight Commander Nicholl and carried by Pigeon N.U.R.P./17/F.16331. The pigeon died of exhaustion shortly after it reached the Norfolk coast. The message reads: 'We have landed to pick up DH4 crew, about 50 E by N of Yarmouth. Sea too rough to get off. Will you please send for us as soon as possible as boat is leaking. We are taxiing W by S.'

The four rescued officers on board HMS *Halcyon* on their way back to Great Yarmouth. From left to right: Trewin (D.H.4), Nicholl, (H.12) Leckie (H.12) and Gilligan (D.H.4). As a sign of the times, the two air mechanics on board the H.12, Thompson and Walker, were not included in photograph.

88

Sound Mirror – Dover, Kent

New technology for early detection of raiding aircraft

The air raids on Britain stimulated experiments in sound location and the first of these took place in July 1915 at Binbury Manor in Kent. A 16 feet diameter parabolic reflector cut into the face of a chalk quarry picked up the sounds of aircraft between 30 seconds and two and a half minutes earlier than an unaided ear but neither the RNAS nor the War Office were convinced enough to adopt the idea.[120]

In 1917 the Munition Inventions Department of the Ministry of Munitions showed renewed

The 1917 sound mirror carved into the cliff at Fan Bay, Dover, and the first to be reported in action during a raid, on 1/2 October 1917. The photo was taken during the recent excavation; the brickwork in front of the mirror relates to a nearby gun battery established in the Second World War.

interest, carving a 15-foot diameter acoustic dish into the chalk cliff at Fan Bay (also known as Fan Hole), Dover, rendering its surface with concrete to provide a smooth reflective surface. A three-foot pivoted trumpet connected to a stethoscope picked up the reflected aircraft engine sound, from which the operator could gauge its bearing and direction.[121]

The Fan Bay sound mirror first saw service during the Gotha raid of 1/2 October 1917 and received a good report from the anti-aircraft commander at Dover:

'An experimental sound detector had been erected at Fan Hole ... in a secluded, sheltered hollow of the ground and proved of great interest and will, I think, be invaluable ... Enemy machines were heard going down Channel past Dover about 12 to 15 miles out to sea and out of the hearing of the Dover guns ... this post promises to be of great value in obtaining information.'[122]

The Fan Bay mirror, alongside another carved out of the cliff in the 1920s, were buried under 600 cubic metres of soil and rubble in the 1970s as part of a programme by the local council to 'clear up' the area. In 2012 the National Trust purchased the land and two years later uncovered the sound mirrors as part of their project to reopen the Second World War Fan Bay tunnels.

A number of sound mirrors were constructed on the north-east coast of England but little is known of their origin. It is often claimed they were built in 1916 but that seems unlikely given their more sophisticated appearance when compared with the 1917 'experimental' mirror at Fan Bay.

The sound mirror at Kilnsea on the east coast of Yorkshire. There is no evidence to show it came into action during the First World War. (Courtesy of Chris Kolonko)

More likely, construction began on the north-east sound mirrors in late 1917 or 1918. There is no record of these sound mirrors reporting the approach of Zeppelins in 1917 or 1918 and, as the last Zeppelin raid took place in April 1918, this may suggest completion after that date.

Another sound mirror on the north-east coast, at Fulwell, north of Sunderland. As with the Kilnsea mirror, there is no evidence it was used to give early warning of air raids in the First World War. (Courtesy of Mark Lawley)

89

The Internal Gangway of Zeppelin L 49

The worst night of the First Blitz for Germany's Naval Zeppelins

In response to Britain's improving aerial defence capability, Germany produced a new class of Zeppelin – starting with the s-class – that, because of their ability to reach heights significantly greater than previous models, became known to the British as the 'Height Climbers'. Germany anticipated these Zeppelins operating beyond the reach of Britain's AA guns and aircraft. On 19 October 1917, a raid by 11 of these latest Zeppelins set out to attack the industrial north of England but, flying at these extreme heights, they ran into a fierce storm blowing from the north-west with speeds up to 50mph. It played havoc with the raiding airships, blowing them wildly off course and forcing them south and south-east. Only six Zeppelins got home in one piece.

Although the commander of Zeppelin L 49 believed he came inland over Yorkshire, blown off course to the south, his bombs actually fell in Norfolk. With two engines out of action, L 49 careered across France at the mercy of the wind. Near Neufchateau, her commander, Kapitänleutnant Hans-Karl Gayer, descended to try to establish his position and then ran into aircraft of France's Escadrille N.152. For the crew of L 49, who had been in the air for about 18 hours, much of the time in sub-zero temperatures, things could not have appeared

A small section of the walkway from the hull of Zeppelin L 49, which was forced down in France after a disastrous raid on England during the night of 19/20 October 1917.

worse. With his reduced engine power, Gayer realised he could not elude the French aircraft, so decided to bring L 49 down before she was shot down. Unknown to him, the French squadron was not armed with explosive and incendiary ammunition.

L 49 landed about three miles from Bourbonne-les-Bains. Although the crew survived their traumatic experience, the presence of an armed mob of French farm workers prevented them destroying their ship. This failure handed the latest Zeppelin design, virtually intact, into the hands of the allies.

Having made detailed plans of the grounded Zeppelin, the French dismantled her before distributing various parts to their allies; some appeared on display in Paris. A small section of the internal gangway of L 49 survives in the Zeppelin Museum, Friedrichshafen. The gangway ran the entire length of a Zeppelin, inside the cloth envelope, allowing the crew to move around the airship. There were no handrails or safety guards. As weight was critical in the 'Height Climbers', only alternate slats made of hollow wooden sections were fitted.

A view from inside a Zeppelin - with the gas cells deflated. A small section of gangway is visible before it passes under the gas cells.

The undignified end of Zeppelin L 49 near Bourbonne-les-Bains in France. All the crew survived the landing but were prevented from destroying their ship before being taken prisoner.

90

Gotha GV 906/16
Rochford, Essex
A valuable prize goes up in smoke

In the early hours of 6 December 1917, *Kagohl* 3 sent 16 Gothas to England, joined in their mission to bomb London by two of the massive *Riesenflugzeug* – 'Giants' – of Rfa 501. Most aircraft carried the new 4.5kg incendiary bomb, which proved largely ineffective.

One of the raiders, Gotha GV, No. 906/16, crewed by its commander, Leutnant R. W. O. Wessels; pilot, Gemeiner J. Rzechtalski; and gunner, Vizefeldwebel O. E. A. Jakobs, approached up the Thames Estuary. When near Canvey Island, anti-aircraft fire from either Bowers Gifford or Hawkesbury Bush shattered the port propeller. Struggling to keep the aircraft aloft, the crew saw landing flares and turned towards them. The flares marked Rochford, home to No. 61 Squadron, RFC. As the Gotha approached, Wessels fired a flare, the colour fortuitously matching the squadron's signal colour of the day; the ground staff acknowledged the flare and the damaged Gotha prepared to land unhindered. Unfortunately, in the dark Rzechtalski failed to notice a tree, which the Gotha hit, throwing it out of control to crash on the Rochford Hundred golf course.

Police Sergeant Rennett heard the aircraft crash at about 5am and, rushing towards the sound, found it surrounded by RFC men helping the crew from the aircraft. He described the aircraft as 'only apparently slightly damaged'.[123] This was a tremendous coup, the first intact Gotha to fall into British hands. Aware that the petrol tanks were leaking and soaking the ground, those present began removing the bombs, of which there were over 60. Others began detaching the engines. The squadron's equipment officer picked up a signal pistol from the wreckage and put it in the pocket of his mackintosh. Cecil Lewis, one of the pilots at Rochford, explains what happened next:

'As he walked away, he pulled it out to show to one of the others. The trigger had no guard, caught in his pocket flap, and the pistol went off. The white-hot magnesium flare bounced along the ground, reached the petrol, and instantly the whole wreckage was in flames. Next morning, only the charred iron-work of the fuselage, the engines and wires were left.'[124]

This took place at about 6.15am. It seems that a few souvenirs were taken from the Gotha before the fire destroyed this valuable prize. One such souvenir, a quarter of a black cross, possibly cut from a wing, resides in the clubhouse of the Rochford Hundred golf course.

A quadrant of a cross cut from Gotha GV 906/16, which was accidentally set on fire on the morning of 6 December 1917, denying a valuable prize to its captors. The inscription identifies it as: 'Gotha No. GO GV 906/16 Brought down and caught fire at Rochford Essex on the 6.12.17 at 4.30am.'

91

Gotha GV 674/16
Near Canterbury, Kent

A small scrap of fabric recovered from a
crashed Gotha

During the Gotha raid on 6 December 1917, bomber GV 674/16 reached the capital, where it dropped 62 of the small 4.5kg incendiary bombs. However, the London AA guns found their mark and a shell fragment damaged the port engine radiator. As the Gotha headed across Kent, the engine gradually overheated, then caught fire. To lighten their aircraft, the crew ditched a machine gun and belt of ammunition, but it was to no avail and the Gotha came down at 5.50am, crashing on a marsh south of Folly Farm, between Hackington and Sturry, north-east of Canterbury.

The engine noise of the descending Gotha alerted a number of people, who then heard a distinct thud as it hit the ground. When some farm hands arrived, the crew, Leutnant Franz R. Schulte (commander), Vizefeldwebel B. Senf (pilot) and Leutnant P. W. Bernard (gunner), were getting out of their flying clothes. One of the officers spoke to them in broken English, 'We German; fetch a constable'.[125] But one of the Germans pointed a revolver at J. B. Wilford, a Red Cross orderly who offered to tend to their injuries, holding him at gunpoint until they had set fire to their aircraft.

The Rev. Philip Somerville of St Stephen's Church, Hackington, also heard the aircraft coming down. As well as serving the church, Somerville was also the senior Special Constable in the area. When flames shot up, he and Special Constable G. W. Haimes ran towards the crash site, where one of the crew announced to Somerville, 'Two German officers and one man'. Having arrested them, Somerville then tended to one of the officers who had suffered an injury, while Haimes searched them for any papers, finding none. Three more Specials then arrived. Leaving one to guard the discarded clothes and another with the burning aircraft, Somerville and two colleagues marched the prisoners away. Meeting two regular policemen on the road who had cycled out from Canterbury, Somerville handed over his prisoners, who were taken to Canterbury Police Station in a passing ambulance. The Specials returned to guard the crash site, which thousands of sightseers visited during the day.[126] The Red Cross collected £32 from them. It had proved quite a day for the Rev. Somerville.

At least one small section of fabric from the Gotha survived the fire and is now in the collection of the RAF Museum at Hendon.

A small section of fabric from Gotha GV 674/16, which survived the fire started by the crew before surrendering to a local Special Constable, Rev. Philip Somerville.

Skeleton of Lower Right-hand Wing
The Remains of the Fabric can be seen

Framework of Aileron or Balancing Flap

Framework of Aileron or Balancing Flap

Framework of Upper Left-hand Wing

The wreckage of a Gotha that crashed on 6 December 1917. Although not specifically identified, because of the terrain I believe this is GV 674/16.

92

10 Stone Buildings – Lincoln's Inn, London

Enduring evidence of bomb damage

On 18 December 1917, the designation of *Kagohl 3 (Kampfgeschwader 3 der OHL)* changed to *Bogohl 3 (Bombengeschwader 3 der OHL)*. On the same day the squadron's temporary commander, Richard Walter, authorised the latest attempt on London. Thirteen Gothas came inland, as did one 'Giant' from *Rfa 501*.

At Lincoln's Inn, one of the Inns of Court, they received a warning of a possible air raid at 6.45pm. At the time, the Masters of the Bench were holding a Council Meeting attended by 26 Benchers. A dinner was due to follow at 7pm but on receipt of this news they delayed it. The call to take cover followed and then, at about 7.30pm, the sound of anti-aircraft guns filled

A view of the damaged wall of No. 10 Stone Buildings, Lincoln's Inn, looking to the left of the entrance.

The damaged wall of No. 10 Stone Buildings to the right of the entrance.

the air. By then the Benchers had adjourned – to the wine cellar. One of them, Sir Arthur Underhill, recalled: 'Someone … suggested that the wine cellar was probably bomb-proof and that there was a barrel of oysters in the larder.' There they 'ate oysters to the accompaniment of champagne'.[127]

The sound of gunfire became constant and bombs fell within a short distance of Lincoln's Inn. A short lull followed and many thought the raid over but, at about 8.10pm, a bomb exploded within the grounds of Lincoln's Inn. The explosion shook the hall and library. When the 'All Clear' sounded at 8.45pm, people ventured outside and found the bomb had exploded in the road outside the drill hall at No. 10 Stone Buildings, formerly the headquarters of the Inns of Court Regiment but home of the Inns of Court Officers' Training Corps since 1913.

The blast smashed windows at Nos. 10–11 Old Square and all along Stone Buildings, where it also 'caused considerable damage to the stone steps and doorway and entrance and to the iron railings. The whole of the window sashes and frames on the west side and many on the east side of the Drill Hall were destroyed and the internal doors and partitions displaced'. The raid over, having enjoyed their appetiser of oysters and champagne, the Benchers returned to the hall for their delayed dinner.

No. 10 Stone Buildings, now headquarters to No. 68 (Inns of Court & City Yeomanry) Signal Squadron, part of No. 71 (Yeomanry) Signal Regiment, still retains much of the damage sustained to its stonework on the evening of 18 December 1917. A small disc set in the tarmac of the road indicates where the bomb exploded.

Some of the damage to No. 10 Stone Buildings and the neighbouring property. In the roadway a disc marks where the bomb exploded.

The brass plaque on Stone Buildings explaining what happened there on 18 December 1917.

THE ROUND STONE IN THE ROADWAY OPPOSITE THIS POINT MARKS THE SPOT WHERE, ON WEDNESDAY THE 18TH DECEMBER 1917, AT 8-10 P.M. A BOMB FROM A GERMAN AEROPLANE STRUCK THE GROUND AND EXPLODED, SHATTERING THE WINDOWS IN STONE BUILDINGS AND DOING OTHER MATERIAL DAMAGE.

93

St Paul's Church
Covent Garden, London
A tribute to a much-loved rector

During a raid on the night of 28/29 January 1918, three or four Gothas reached London, as did a single *Riesenflugzeug* – 'Giant' aircraft. Following the warning of an impending raid, hundreds made their way to the Odhams Printing Works in Long Acre, Covent Garden, to the east of Endell Street, where the owners had made their huge basement area available as a shelter. It was a popular shelter as 'people knew they would be well looked after and provided with refreshments'.[128]

The last Gotha dropped its bombs over north-west London around 10pm, but no 'All Clear' notice followed. It must have seemed frustrating to those sheltering at Odhams as midnight approached, but the authorities were still tracking the movements of German aircraft. At 12.15am, R.12, the 'Giant', reached the capital, dropping its first bombs over Bethnal Green. Heading south, R.12 crossed the River Thames, then recrossed it near Waterloo Bridge, heading towards Covent Garden, where it released a massive 300kg high-explosive bomb. It smashed down through the pavement lights of Odhams to explode in the basement.

The devastation and destruction caused by the bomb was immense. It took some six weeks

The commemorative door on the north wall of St Paul's Church, Covent Garden.

The destruction caused at Odhams Printing Works, used during raids as a public shelter. Thirty-eight of those taking cover in the basement were killed and 85 injured.

before rescue workers managed to recover the last of the bodies from the rubble, giving a final tally of 38 dead and 85 injured, the most casualties caused in London by a single bomb.

One victim was the Rev. Edward Henry Mosse, aged 61, the rector of St Paul's Church. His son explained at the inquest that his father went out that night 'to visit the parish, as he always did during an air raid. He had been to several houses and shelters, and was leaving another, when a bomb fell.'[129] Another report says that Mosse went out to search for three children separated from their mother. Having found them he took them back to her at Odhams and was about to leave to visit other parishioners when the bomb dropped.[130]

In a tribute to Rev. Mosse, the Bishop of London reflected on how, 'The afterglow of a beautiful life would hang over Covent Garden for years.' After the war a bronze plaque was added to the door on the north side of St Paul's Church to commemorate his death, which occurred 'while ministering to his people'. His name also appears on the war memorial in the grounds of St Luke's Church, Heage, Derbyshire, the village where Mosse grew up.

The inscription on the door of St Paul's Church commemorating Rev. Edward Henry Mosse, killed when a 300kg bomb dropped by 'Giant' R.12 destroyed Odhams Printing Works in Long Acre, Covent Garden. (Historic Military Press)

94

Gatehouse Clock
Kew Bridge Waterworks, London
Destroyed by a bomb but restored to working order

On the night after the raid that caused such loss of life in Covent Garden, three of the massive *Riesenflugzeug* attacked England; for the first time they did so without the Gothas of *Bogohl 3*.

Only one of the 'Giants' reached London – R.39, built by the Zeppelin works at Staaken. Having skirted around the capital, its commander, Hauptmann Richard von Bentivegni – who was also the squadron commander of *Rfa 501* – thought he had identified Tower Bridge and commenced an attack that he believed would strike the docks. In fact the bridge he saw was Hammersmith Bridge, seven miles west of Tower Bridge, and the ten bombs he dropped on what he must have thought were the docks, fell in and around the reservoirs at the Kew Bridge Waterworks and in the neighbouring streets.

The most lethal bomb of the ten exploded on the Waterworks' main gatehouse, where the foremen had an office. The bomb wrecked the office, killing both engine foreman Frederick William Finch and district foreman George Bentley.

Protected by a small porch, a clock hung on the front face of this gatehouse. This was a replacement for an earlier clock, put in place

The restored clock originally destroyed by a bomb dropped on the Kew Bridge Waterworks shortly before midnight on the evening of 29 January 1918 by 'Giant' R.39.

around 1890. No doubt many members of staff had checked the time nervously in the intervening years when passing it as they clocked on for work. The bomb blast destroyed both the clock and wall of the gatehouse. In the aftermath, Richard Thomas Kemish, a talented employee at the waterworks, serving there from 1902 until his retirement in 1931, asked for and received permission to collect up the pieces of the shattered clock. Kemish sifted through the rubble and gathered up all the pieces he could find, then began to engineer replacement parts for those missing and got the clock working again. He built a new, floral-patterned, wooden case for it and proudly displayed it in his home.[131] Kemish died in 1941, aged 75. The clock stayed in the possession of the family until 1970, when Kemish's daughter donated it to the Metropolitan Water Board. The site of the Kew Bridge Waterworks is now home to the London Museum of Water & Steam; Richard Thomas Kemish's restored bomb-ravaged clock now sits on the wall in the café area but sadly, at the time of writing, has no label explaining its remarkable story.

The shattered foremen's office by the gatehouse of the Kew Bridge Waterworks. The clock hung on the front face of the gatehouse. (Courtesy of London Museum of Water & Steam/Thames Water Archive)

95

The Kerley Family Grave
South Ealing Cemetery, London

Tragic loss of a London family

Before 'Giant' R.39 dropped its bombs over the Kew Bridge Waterworks, it had approached over Richmond Old Deer Park and Syon House, dropping a number of bombs, which caused little damage. Over Brentford, however, all that changed.

A local man, George Bentley (not the same George Bentley killed at the waterworks), was walking home at 11.35pm when he saw the 'Giant' held by a searchlight. 'At the same moment a man a few yards in front of me dived to the ground and shouted to me to lie down, which I did … There were three deafening thuds and flashes.'[132]

One bomb exploded near his house. Bentley found all the windows and doors smashed but those inside, both his baby daughter and an aunt, were unharmed. He then went to nearby Whitestile Road, where another bomb had fallen. His worst fears were realised when

The sad death toll of the Kerley family as a result of a bomb dropped on Whitestile Road, Brentford. It claimed the lives of Sergeant-Major Kerley's wife, his five children and a niece. (Courtesy of Robert Mitchell)

he reached No. 22, the home of his friend, Herbert Kerley, a sergeant-major in the Middlesex Regiment. The house lay in ruins. Bentley realised that his friend's wife and children must have been inside. Then he heard a groan. Despite the danger, Bentley began to pull at the rubble. 'I pulled and wriggled my way into the cellar, which was full of gas and water, and in the darkness came across a young woman, only just alive. Most of her clothes were blown off. With help I managed to get her to the surface, but by that time she was dead.'

The young woman was 22-year-old Hilda Kerley, Sergeant-Major Kerley's niece. It was not until the following afternoon that rescuers recovered the last body. It was as Bentley had feared. As well as his niece, Herbert Kerley's wife, May, was dead, as were his children: Florence aged twelve, Henry, eight, Lilian, five, Daisy, three, and little Ellen, just three months old. There was one more body, bringing the death toll to eight: Catherine Berrows, aged 70, the Kerleys' lodger. Herbert Kerley, bereaved husband and father lived on without his family until June 1944.

In previous raids, bombs had frequently killed two or three members of the same family, occasionally four, five or six. There are two instances of seven: the Kerley family and also the Tyler family in Sheffield, killed during a Zeppelin raid in September 1916. The most is eight; this unwelcome distinction belongs to the Kingston family (seven siblings and their cousin) in Hither Green, killed during a Zeppelin raid in October 1917.

The extensive damage inflicted on the Kerley's house at 22 Whitestile Road meant that when it was rebuilt it was done so in a plainer, simpler style. (Courtesy of Robert Mitchell)

96

The Royal Hospital
Chelsea, London
The first 1,000kg bomb strike

On the night of 16 February 1918, five of the Staaken 'Giants' set out for London but encountered high winds on route. Three settled for secondary targets nearer the coast while two pushed on to the capital. One had an unsettling encounter with the balloon apron protecting the eastern approaches to London before turning for home, leaving just one 'Giant' to reach the city.

Since its raid over the Kew Bridge Waterworks the previous month, 'Giant' R.39 had undergone modification to allow it to carry a single 1,000kg bomb, the largest type dropped from the air during the war. Over London, the commander of

The north-east wing of the Royal Hospital Chelsea. First destroyed on 16 February when a German 'Giant' dropped the first 1,000kg bomb on London. It was rebuilt, but destroyed again by a V2 rocket in the Second World War. The building retains its original appearance.

R.39, Richard von Bentivegni, believed they were just east of the financial heart of the City when he released the bomb shortly after 10pm. But, as in his raid on Kew, he was much further west than he had anticipated, and his bomb hurtled down to strike the north-east wing of the Royal Hospital, the home of the Chelsea Pensioners. This wing housed the three officers holding the position Captain of Invalids and their families. One of them, Ernest Ludlow, a former Grenadier Guards officer, lived there with his wife Jessie, their five sons, and a niece, Alice Copley.

The bomb smashed through the roof and down through two floors of the building to explode on the stone cellar floor. The blast seared through the building, the upward force obliterating part of the wing. An eyewitness reported the building 'was sliced in half ... and literally crumbled to dust'.[133] Captain Ludlow died, as did his wife, two of his sons and Alice Copley. Incredibly, the other three sons, the youngest just six months old, were pulled alive from the wreckage.

After the war, a rebuilt north-east wing, constructed in the original style, opened in 1921, but had the misfortune to be destroyed again by a German V2 rocket in January 1945. Five people died in this attack, one of them was Geoffrey Bailey, Captain of Invalids, a role he had fulfilled for many years. He had been in the building but survived when the bomb destroyed it in 1918, only to be killed in the same place 27 years later.

After the war, the wing was rebuilt for a second time, opened by the then Prime Minister, Harold Wilson, in January 1966.

A photograph showing the damage inflicted on the north-east wing of the Royal Hospital in February 1918. The explosion has obliterated the whole side of the building to the right of the central entrance, which houses the Captains of Invalids and their families. (Courtesy of Royal Hospital, Chelsea)

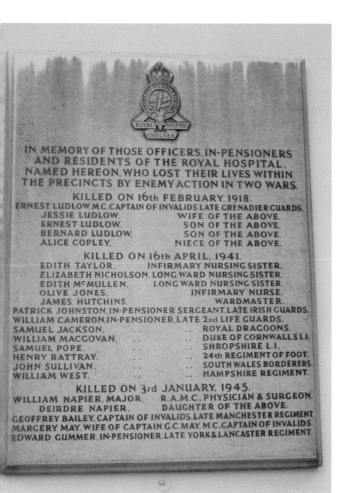

IN MEMORY OF THOSE OFFICERS, IN-PENSIONERS
AND RESIDENTS OF THE ROYAL HOSPITAL,
NAMED HEREON, WHO LOST THEIR LIVES WITHIN
THE PRECINCTS BY ENEMY ACTION IN TWO WARS.

KILLED ON 16th FEBRUARY, 1918.
ERNEST LUDLOW, M.C. CAPTAIN OF INVALIDS, LATE GRENADIER GUARDS.
JESSIE LUDLOW,   WIFE OF THE ABOVE.
ERNEST LUDLOW,   SON OF THE ABOVE.
BERNARD LUDLOW,   SON OF THE ABOVE.
ALICE COPLEY,   NIECE OF THE ABOVE.

KILLED ON 16th APRIL, 1941.
EDITH TAYLOR,   INFIRMARY NURSING SISTER.
ELIZABETH NICHOLSON, LONG WARD NURSING SISTER.
EDITH McMULLEN,   LONG WARD NURSING SISTER.
OLIVE JONES,   INFIRMARY NURSE.
JAMES HUTCHINS,   WARDMASTER.
PATRICK JOHNSTON, IN-PENSIONER SERGEANT, LATE IRISH GUARDS.
WILLIAM CAMERON, IN-PENSIONER, LATE 2nd LIFE GUARDS.
SAMUEL JACKSON, ... ROYAL DRAGOONS.
WILLIAM MACGOVAN, ... DUKE OF CORNWALL'S L.I.
SAMUEL POPE, ... SHROPSHIRE L.I.
HENRY RATTRAY, ... 24th REGIMENT OF FOOT.
JOHN SULLIVAN, ... SOUTH WALES BORDERERS.
WILLIAM WEST, ... HAMPSHIRE REGIMENT.

KILLED ON 3rd JANUARY, 1945.
WILLIAM NAPIER, MAJOR,   R.A.M.C. PHYSICIAN & SURGEON.
DEIRDRE NAPIER,   DAUGHTER OF THE ABOVE.
GEOFFREY BAILEY, CAPTAIN OF INVALIDS, LATE MANCHESTER REGIMENT.
MARGERY MAY, WIFE OF CAPTAIN G.C. MAY, M.C. CAPTAIN OF INVALIDS.
EDWARD GUMMER, IN-PENSIONER, LATE YORK & LANCASTER REGIMENT.

A plaque inside the grounds of the Royal Hospital commemorating those killed there in two world wars. At the top are those killed on 16 February 1918. Near the bottom is the name of Geoffrey Bailey. Although in the building when the bomb struck in February 1918, he survived, but was killed when a V2 rocket struck in January 1945.

A massive 1,000kg high-explosive bomb, the type that struck the Royal Hospital and the heaviest dropped from the air during the First World War.

97

F.E.2b Tail Boom
Annfield Plain, County Durham
Remembering a Home Defence pilot killed in a flying accident

On 13 March 1918, three navy Zeppelins set out for a raid aimed at the industrial Midlands, but a significant change in wind direction resulted in their recall. Two followed orders, L 42 did not.

Commanded by Kapitänleutnant Martin Dietrich, L 42 arrived unobserved over West Hartlepool, attacked the town, and was away just after 9.30pm. Warned of a possible raid, three aircraft from No. 36 Squadron, RFC, took off between 8.10 and 8.20pm, as did one from No. 76 Squadron. By 9.15pm three more from No. 36 Squadron were in the air. One of these, an F.E.2b (A5470), had Pilot Sergeant Arthur John Joyce at the controls. He took off from the airfield at Hylton, near Sunderland, to patrol a line from Cramlington to Easington, searching for the raiders. At 10.45pm Joyce got into difficulties and onlookers saw him circling the high point of Pontop Pike before crashing on sloping ground near Annfield Plain, County Durham.[134] On hitting the ground, the F.E.2b burst into flames and Joyce died in the wreckage of his aircraft – one of many accidental air crew casualties of the First Blitz.

Arthur Joyce was a Londoner, working on the railways before the war, and had married Florence in 1913. They had two children, Muriel born in 1916 and a son, Dennis Arthur, only two months old. Although not from the area, his death moved the local residents.

The community opened a fund to build a memorial in his honour, with much of the final amount made up of the pennies of ordinary working people. The monument, in the form

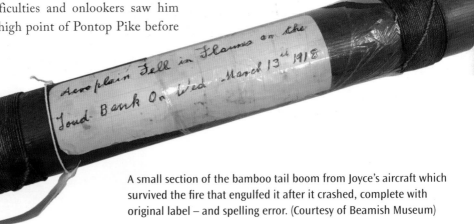

A small section of the bamboo tail boom from Joyce's aircraft which survived the fire that engulfed it after it crashed, complete with original label – and spelling error. (Courtesy of Beamish Museum)

of an obelisk, was unveiled opposite Loud Terrace in Annfield Plain on 14 May 1919 before a crowd of about 3,000 people. A shield on the obelisk bears the words: 'It was here Sergt Joyce met his death on the night of March 13th 1918.' Below that, on the base, is the following inscription: 'This monument is erected by the inhabitants of Annfield Plain and District in grateful recognition of this gallant airman's great sacrifice. In his own words, "our lives are not our own, they belong to our country".'[135]

Tragically, Joyce's son, Dennis, died in September 1940 while on a bombing mission over Germany with No. 44 Squadron, RAF. His name was added to his father's memorial during its refurbishment in 1959.

A small section of the bamboo tail boom from Joyce's wrecked F.E.2b has recently come to light in storage at the Beamish Museum.

Three weeks before his fatal crash, Joyce had survived a bad landing. Here he is standing in the cockpit of the F.E.2b, which lost its undercarriage in the landing. The bamboo tail booms are visible, extending behind the wings. (Courtesy of Cross and Cockade International (CCI))

The Sergeant Joyce memorial in Annfield Plain, County Durham, funded by contributions from local people. (Courtesy of Rob Langham)

The inscription on the memorial, under an RAF eagle. Although Joyce was flying as a pilot of the RFC at the time of his death, the RAF came into being 19 days later. (Courtesy of Rob Langham)

Damaged Milestone
Bold Heath, Lancashire

Evidence of the final Zeppelin raid of the
First Blitz

The last Zeppelin raid to drop bombs on British soil took place on the night of 12/13 April 1918. Of the five Zeppelins that took part, L 61 reached the furthest point west of any Zeppelin during the war – coming within 12 miles of Liverpool.

Kapitänleutnant Herbert Ehrlich, commanding L 61, came inland over the Yorkshire coast near Withernsea at 9.30pm. He crossed the Humber and headed west, passing a few miles south of Doncaster and Sheffield, but had by then become lost to ground observation. Heading north-west, L 61 crossed the River Mersey near Widnes and reappeared over Bold Heath in Lancashire at about 11.10pm. Something here attracted his attention and Ehrlich dropped two 50kg high-explosive bombs.

Dr Henry Bates, the Mayor of St Helens, lived not far from where the bombs fell. They woke Bates' wife, who thought someone was trying to break into the house. A telephone call then alerted Bates that it was an air raid. In a letter to a friend he explained there had been two very loud explosions, which shook the doors and windows, and about ten or eleven in the distance:

'Two bombs were dropped in this neighbourhood, one between a munition works and Clockface colliery … The other on the main road between Bold Heath and Rainhill … The telegraph wires were all out in two sections and the poles damaged. A large hole sufficient to hold a small cottage was made in the main road, and the Widnes water main burst. The contents from the hole were blown into an adjoining field, the hedge all scorched and the windows in some houses about 200 yards away smashed.'[136]

After these two bombs, L 61 headed towards Wigan and carried out the main attack, providing the source of the distant explosions heard by Bates and his wife.

Back at the hamlet of Bold Heath, as well as the damage described by Henry Bates, the bomb also smashed the front portion of a milestone, on the midway point between Warrington and Prescot on the road that is now the A57.

At some point workmen removed the damaged milestone to Widnes and it went on display in Victoria Park. Later, however, it ended up in a maintenance yard at the park and was forgotten until rediscovery about 40 years ago, after which it was put back on display in the park alongside detailed information plaques written by local historian Peter J. C. Smith.[137]

The milestone that once stood at Bold Heath, on the main road (now the A57) between Warrington and Prescot. The explosion of the bomb cut away part of the face of the milestone. (Courtesy of Gerry Ryder, www.RainhillRemembers.uk)

After going missing for a number of years, the milestone is now on public display in Victoria Park, Widnes, with two plaques explaining its history. (Courtesy of Gerry Ryder, www.RainhillRemembers.uk)

The command gondola of L 61 prior to entering service with the Naval Airship Division. The electric switches controlling the release of bombs were positioned in the command gondola.

99

An Unexploded British Anti-Aircraft Shell

The forgotten casualties of the First Blitz

The last raid that reached Britain took place on the night of 19/20 May 1918. With 41 attacking aircraft – 38 Gothas and three 'Giants' – it proved the largest of the First Blitz. But in the last year of the war Britain's air defences had taken a major step forward and London now had an integrated defence system bringing together the aircraft, guns, searchlights, balloon aprons and observers that protected the capital into the London Air Defence Area (LADA), all under a single commander. Of the 41 raiders it appears that only 18 battled through the defences to reach the capital. Home Defence aircraft shot down three Gothas, another made a forced landing in Essex and the anti-aircraft guns brought down two more off the coast. For many of the new and inexperienced German crews the intense anti-aircraft barrage proved too much, releasing their bombs over Kent and Essex and turning for home. The difference between the AA barrages fired during the first London daytime Gotha raid in June 1917 and this raid in May 1918 was marked. In the June 1917 raid the London guns had fired 360 rounds; in this last raid the LADA guns fired over 30,000 rounds into the night sky.

This volume of artillery shells fired into the air, however, created a problem on the ground, because what goes up must come down. From the earliest Zeppelin raids the British authorities had resisted the demands for an air raid warning system in London. An unexpected result of the air raids was that many rushed outside to watch them, endangering themselves and potentially obstructing the emergency services. Out in the streets these people had no protection from flying bomb fragments or falling anti-aircraft shells. The Government felt, however, that if a warning of a raid was given even more people would go outside to watch, when its aim was to keep people indoors during raids. Only after public agitation following the second daylight Gotha raid on the capital on 7 July 1917 did London get a warning system, over two years after the first Zeppelin raid.

The anti-aircraft shells that fell over London varied enormously in size, from complete unexploded shells to fragments of all shapes and sizes. An attempt was made to compile separate lists of damage caused by falling shells during the period of the Gotha and 'Giant' raids and it appears that over 2,400 properties suffered to a greater or lesser extent. Most often this damage consisted of broken roofs, damaged ceilings and smashed windows. But there was another cost too – that in human lives. The records attribute at least 23 deaths and 182 injuries in London due to falling British shells. Inevitably, similar incidents occurred all over the country. It is an often overlooked aspect of this First Blitz, but it is one that should be recognised.

This unexploded 3-inch 20 cwt shell was fired during a raid on Chatham in Kent on 30 September 1917 and landed in the dockyard. This part of the shell weighs 5lb (2.2kg) and would easily have smashed through the roof of any building it struck. It is currently in the collection of the Historic Dockyard, Chatham. (Historic Military Press)

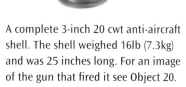

A complete 3-inch 20 cwt anti-aircraft shell. The shell weighed 16lb (7.3kg) and was 25 inches long. For an image of the gun that fired it see Object 20.

100

Grave Markers, German Military Cemetery Cannock Chase, Staffordshire

The last resting place of the fallen raiders

When the air war over Britain ended, the crews of those German airships and aeroplanes shot down and killed while over the country lay in graves near to where they died. This meant that the crews of both SL 11 and L 31 were interred side-by-side in St Mary's cemetery in Mutton Lane, Potter's Bar, that of L 32 in the graveyard at St Mary Magdalene, Great Burstead, and L 48 at a small cemetery opposite St Peter's Church, Theberton. Six unidentified bodies of crewmen from L 34, shot down off the coast at Hartlepool in November 1916, washed up along the north-east coast in January 1917 and were buried in local cemeteries. Likewise, crews of Gothas killed over England were buried locally.

Many years later, in October 1959, the British and German Governments made an agreement as to the future care of the remains of those German servicemen and internees from both world wars who had died in Britain. The agreement led to the creation of a single

The stone slabs in the Zeppelin enclosure at Cannock Chase German Cemetery that mark the final resting places of each of the airship crews shot down over Britain.

cemetery on six acres of land at Cannock Chase in Staffordshire, where all the remains not already under the care of the Commonwealth War Graves Commission, would be transferred. The German War Graves Commission (*Volksbund Deutsche Kriegsgraberfursorge*) arranged to move the remains from 706 scattered burials. The inauguration and dedication of the new cemetery, containing the remains of almost 5,000 German and Austrian bodies, took place on 10 June 1967.[138] Unfortunately vandals daubed red paint on dozens of the graves a few hours before the opening ceremony but the efforts of 15 young Germans assisted by local volunteers removed most before the guests arrived.[139]

The crews of the four German airships lay in a walled area to the side of the entrance hall. There are four large stone slabs, one for each airship, bearing the names of those killed. Behind them stands a stone bearing these words in German and English:

'Side by side with their comrades, the crews of four Zeppelins shot down over England during the First World War here found their eternal resting place. The fallen were brought here from their original burial places at Potters Bar, Great Burstead and Theberton. The members of each crew are buried in caskets in one grave.'

These German airmen, like the British airmen who went up to oppose them, were all pioneers in this new age of aerial warfare. They are at once protagonists and victims of this First, forgotten Blitz.

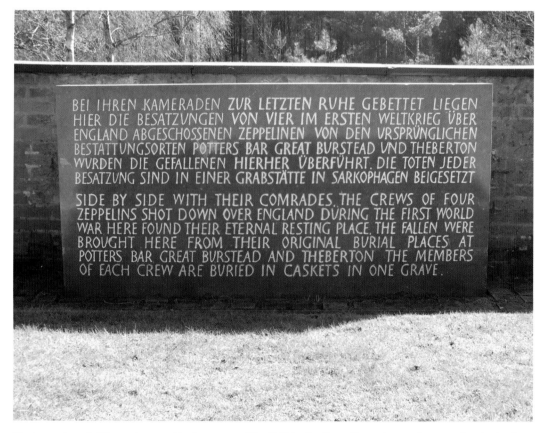

The large stone (with words carved in German and English) in the Zeppelin enclosure that contains the bodies of the airship crews of SL 11, L 31, L 32 and L 48. The Sussex sculptor John Skelton designed the stone and cut the inscriptions.

This stone slab lies over the grave of the crew of Zeppelin L 32, giving the names and rank of each member of the crew buried beneath it.

Before moving to Cannock, the Zeppelin crews were buried close to where their airships fell. This postcard shows the original burial place of the crew of L 32 in the churchyard of St Mary Magdalene at Great Burstead, Essex.

Endnotes

1. Robinson, Douglas H., *The Zeppelin in Combat – A History of the German Naval Airship Division 1912–1918*, (Atglen, Pennsylvania: Schiffer Military/Aviation History, 1994), p. 56.

2. *Official History of the Ministry of Munitions* – Vol. X, Part VI (Anti-Aircraft Supplies), (Uckfield, East Sussex: Naval & Military Press Ltd (facsimile reprint), 2009), p. 24.

3. https://www.iwm.org.uk/collections/item/object/30025222

4. Jones, H. A., *The War in the Air – Being the Story of The Part Played in the Great War by the Royal Air Force*, Vol. III, (Oxford: Clarendon Press, 1931), pp. 78–79.

5. The Times Digital Archive (TDA), *The Times*, 26 December 1914, p. 7.

6. Wyatt, R. J., *Death From the Skies – The Zeppelin Raids over Norfolk, 19 January 1915*, (Norwich: Gliddon Books, 1990), pp. 12–13, 43–48.

7. Ibid, p. 22.

8. TDA, *The Times*, 22 January 1915, p. 34.

9. Robinson, op. cit. p. 78.

10. The National Archives (TNA), AIR1/569/16/15/137.

11. Austen, Chas. A. F., *Ramsgate Raid Records*, (Ramsgate: Michael's Bookshop – reprint 2006 – first published circa 1919), p. 11.

12. Easdown, Martin & Genth, Thomas, *A Glint in the Sky – German First World War Air Attacks on Folkestone, Dover, Ramsgate, Margate & Other Kentish Towns*, (Barnsley, Pen & Sword Local, 2004), p. 122.

13. Morison, Frank, *War on Great Cities – A Study of the Facts*, (London, Faber and Faber, 1937), pp. 40–41.

14. Robinson, op. cit. p. 96.

15. Mansfield, F. A., *History of Gravesend in the County of Kent*, (Gravesend: Gravesend & Dartford Reporter, 1922), p. 154.

16. TNA, AIR1/569/16/15/142.

17. TDA, *The Times*, 12 July 1916, p. 5.

18. North East War Memorials Project (NEWMP), www.newmp.org.uk/detail.php?contentId=7786

19. TDA, *The Times*, 14 July 1915, p. 10.

20. Daily Telegraph WW1 Archive, *Daily Telegraph*, 10 November 1915, p. 9.

21. TDA, *The Times*, 6 November 1917, p. 7.

22. https://historicengland.org.uk/listing/the-list/list-entry/1427535

23. Robinson, op. cit. p. 124.

24. TNA, AIR1/2417/303/41, *London Evening News*, 1 March 1935.

25. London Metropolitan Archives (LMA), LCC/FB/WAR/03/001-002, London Fire Brigade Reports.

26. TDA, *The Times*, 14 September 1915, p. 8.

27. Robinson, op. cit. p. 127.

28. British Newspaper Archive (BNA), *Leeds Mercury*, 7 August 1916, p. 2.

29. www.derehamhistory.com/1915---zeppelin-raid-on-dereham.html

30. *Eastern Daily Press*, 30 December 1918.

31. Jones, op. cit. pp. 87–88.

32. TNA, WO 158/936, Air Raids, 1915 – Airship Raids, August – September 1915, p. 32.

33. TNA, WO 158/937, Air Raids, 1915 – 13–14 October 1915, p. 14.

34. *Thanet's Raid History*, (Ramsgate: The Thanet Advertiser, 1918 – reprinted Ramsgate: Michael's Bookshop), p. 4.

35. Jones, op. cit. pp. 127–128.

36. Breithaupt, Kapitänleutnant, *How We Bombed London*, (The Living Age, Vol. 334, No. 4322, 15 January 1928), pp. 170–174.

37. TNA, AIR1/572/16/15/153 parts 1 and 2.

38. TNA, AIR1/2417/303/42, *London Evening News*, 19 February 1935.

39. Ibid, 6 February 1935.

40. The Black Books, Vol. VI, 1914–1965 (Lincoln's Inn: The Records of the Honorable Society of Lincoln's Inn, 2001), pp. 257–258.

41. Robinson, op. cit. p. 130.

42. TNA, AIR1/572/16/15/153, part 1.

43. TDA, *The Times*, 24 January 1916, p. 8.

44. Dover and the European War 1914–18, (Dover: Dover Express, 1919), p. 18.

45. TDA, *The Times*, 23 February 1916, p. 5.

46. Long, David, *Night of the Zeppelin - The German airship raid on Loughborough*, (Loughborough: Reprintuk, 2016), p. 34.

47. Ibid, pp. 44–47.

48. https://www.derbyporcelain.org.uk/zeppelin-mark-centenary

49. http://themanchesters.org/forum/index.php?topic=7407.0

50. LMA, COL/SJ/05/003 Correspondence and reports in connection with the compilation of Dr Thomas's 'Activities of the Lord Mayor and the corporation during the Great War'.

51. TNA, AIR1/2301/215/6, Bomb Dart Explosive, Ranken Dart.

52. TNA, AIR1/575/16/15/162, Raids 31 March–1 April 1916.

53. Essex Countryside magazine, Vol. 18, Number 165, October 1970, p. 61.

54. http://sussexhistoryforum.co.uk/index.php?topic=1825.0;wap2

55. TNA, AIR1/576/16/15/164, Air Raids 2/3 April 1916, Edinburgh City Police Report.

56. Conversations with the McLaren family.

57. Robinson, op. cit. pp. 157–158 (Zeppelin commander's observations).

58. TNA, WO158/941, Air Raids 1916 – 24 April/3 May 1916, p. 18.

59. TNA, WO158/941, Air Raids 1916 – 24 April/3 May 1916, p. 19.

60. Cole, Christopher, & Cheesman, E. F., *The Air Defence of Britain 1914–1918*, (London: Bodley Head Ltd, 1984), pp. 105–106.

61. Robinson, op. cit. pp. 171–172.

62. Ibid, p. 385.

63. Cole & Cheesman, op. cit. pp. 143 & 145.

64. Ibid, pp. 149–150.

65. Ibid, p. 167.

66. Ibid, pp. 198–199.

67. ibid, pp. 203 & 205.

68. https://www.iwm.org.uk/collections/item/object/70000215

69. Reay, Colonel W. T., *The Specials – How They Served London*, (London: William Heinemann, 1920), pp. 175–176.

70. Lehmann, Captain Ernest A., and Mingos, Howard, *The Zeppelins – The Development of the Airship, with the Story of the Zeppelin Air Raids in the World War*, (London: G. P. Putnam's Sons, 1927), p. 45.

71. TNA, AIR1/582/16/15/181 part 1, Air Raid 2/3 Sept. 1916.

72. Department of Special Collections, McFarlin Library, The University of Tulsa – letter from WLR to H. Scott Orr.

73. TDA, *The Times*, 28 September 1916, p. 11.

74. Ibid, 29 September 1916, p. 9.

75. Ibid, 5 October 1916, p. 8.

76. http://hartfordhundred.org.uk/essendon.html

77. Essex Record Office, Essex Police Records, First World War, J/P 12/7.

78. https://www.isle-of-wight-fhs.co.uk/articles/burland20080801.html

79. BNA, *Essex Newsman*, 21 October 1916, p. 5.

80. TNA, AIR1/584/16/15/184, *Daily Telegraph*, 27 September 1916.

81. *Sheffield Independent*, 3 December 1918, pp. 1 and 3.

82. Tempest, Major W. J., *How I Shot Down L.31*, The Great War – I Was There, (London: Amalgamated Press, 1939), Part 22, pp. 870–873.

83. Klein, Pitt, *Achtung! Bomben Fallen*, (Leipzig: R. F. Koehler, 1934), pp. 144–145 (English translation by Alastair Reid, privately published as *Bombs Away! Zeppelin at War*, 2016, p. 101).

84. TNA, *The Times*, 3 October 1916, p. 9.

85. MacDonagh, Michael, *In London During the Great War – The Diary of a Journalist*, (London: Eyre & Spottiswoode, 1935), p. 138.

86. Bennett, J.E., *The Potters Bar Zeppelin 2nd October 1916*, (Potters Bar & District Historical Society, 1989), p. 7.

87. Ibid, p. 31.

88. TNA, AIR1/16/15/186 part 1, Air Raid 27/28 November 1916.

89. Ibid.

90. Ibid.

91. Details of actions by No. 37 Squadron complied from Cole & Cheesman.

92. https://historicengland.org.uk/listing/the-list/list-entry/1406155

93. Easdown & Genth, op. cit. pp. 62–63.

94. http://www.leshaigh.co.uk/folkestone/stokesinfo.html

95. Mückler, Jörg, *Deutsche Bomber Im Ersten Weltkreig*, (Stuttgart: Motorbuch Verlag, 2017), p. 117.

96. Ibid, p. 137.

97. TNA, AIR1/2126/207/79/48, English translation of Major Hilmer von Bülow's 1927 report, pp. 22–23.

98. TNA, AIR1/588/16/15/198, Air Raid 5 June 1917.

99. https://www.rafmuseum.org.uk/documents/collections/82-A-1067-Sopwith-Pup-N5182.pdf

100. Cole & Cheesman, op. cit. p. 232.

101. Ibid, p. 238.

102. LMA, CLA/041/IQ/04, City of London Inquest, 13 June 1917.

103. LMA, LCC/FB/WAR/03/001-002, London Fire Brigade Reports.

104. https://www.europeana.eu/portal/en/record/2020601/contributions_7661.html

105. TDA, *The Times*, 16 June 1917, p. 4.

106. Ibid, 21 June 1917, p. 3.

107. Rimell, R. L., *The Last Flight of the L48*, (Berkhamsted: Albatros Productions, 2006), pp. 14–16.

108. Faulkner, Dr Neil, and Durrani, Dr Nadia, *In Search of the Zeppelin War – The Archaeology of the First Blitz*, (Stroud: Tempus Publishing, 2008), pp. 38–45 and 133–143.

109. TDA, *The Times*, 21 June 1917, p. 3.

110. TNA, AIR1/2417/303/42, *London Evening News*, 2 March 1935.

111. Ibid, 25 February 1915.

112. Morison, op. cit. pp.130–131.

113. Chapman, Peter, *Eagle Over England – Leutnant Adolf Genth*, (The '14 '18 Journal, 2010), and discussions with Thomas Genth, grandson of Adolf Genth.

114. TDA, *The Times*, 11 July 1917, p. 7.

115. TNA, AIR1/591/16/15/206, Aeroplane Raid, 22 August 1917.

116. Fegan, Thomas, *The 'Baby Killers' – German Air Raids on Britain in the First World War*, (Barnsley: Leo Cooper, 2002), pp. 57–58.

117. TNA, AIR1/2417/303/42, *London Evening News*, 15 February 1935.

118. TDA, *The Times*, 7 September 1917, p. 3.

119. Snowden Gamble, C. F., *The Story of a North Sea Air Station*, (London: Neville Spearman, reprint 1967), pp. 261–271.

120. Cole & Cheesman, op. cit., p. 46.

121. Ibid, pp. 313–314.

122. TNA, AIR1/595/16/15/216, Air raids on England, 1 October 1917.

123. TNA, AIR1/598/16/15/221, Air Raids on England, 6 December 1917.

124. Lewis, Cecil, *Sagittarius Rising*, (First published 1936, this edition London: Warner Books, 1993), pp. 230–231.

125. TDA, *The Times*, 7 December 1917, p. 9.

126. TNA, AIR1/598/16/15/221, Air Raids on England, 6 December 1917.

127. https://www.lincolnsinn.org.uk/index.php/library/the-inns-archives/archive-of-the-month/aotm-2017/820-air-raid-1917

128. TDA, *The Times*, 4 February 1918, p. 3.

129. TDA, *The Times*, 2 February 1918, p. 3.

130. https://www.militaryimages.net/media/heage-war-memorial-derbyshire.74519/

131. https://www.waterandsteam.org.uk/latest-news/in-remembrance-the-first-world-war-bombing-raid-on-the-kew-bridge-waterworks

132. TNA, AIR1/2417/303/42, *London Evening News*, 5 February 1935.

133. Information received from the Heritage Manager, Royal Hospital, Chelsea.

134. Cole & Cheesman, op. cit. pp. 409–410.

135. www.newmp.org.uk/detail.php?contentId=6280

136. *Zeppelin Attack at Bold*, https://www.suttonbeauty.org.uk/suttonhistory/suttonwar1

137. Smith, Peter J.C., *Zeppelins Over Lancashire*, (Stoneclough: Neil Richardson, 1991), p. 24.

138. TDA, *The Times*, 8 June 1967, p. 3.

139. TDA, *The Times*, 12 June 1967, p. 3.

Index